Keep your eyes
on the grou...
Good luc...
...

D1239350

SHED HUNTING

A GUIDE TO FINDING WHITE-TAILED DEER ANTLERS

JOE SHEAD

Library of Congress Catalog Number: 2006910215
ISBN: 0-9765199-4-1

Shed Antler Press
W3317 South Road
Berlin, WI 54923

Designed by Deb Salzer

Printed by Signature Press
P.O. Box 274
Amherst Junction, WI 54407
(800) 472-5433

Contents

About the Author VI

Acknowledgments VII

Introduction...IX

Chapter 1: The Science of Antlers.................................15

Chapter 2: Find the Bucks First 27

Chapter 3: Equipment and Preparation 45

Chapter 4: Seeking Fallen Bone 53

Chapter 5: You Found One!...87

Chapter 6: Alternative Methods....................................111

Chapter 7: Competition 127

Chapter 8: Antler Roundup...141

References 151

Index..152

Shed Hunting Log..156

"Antlers are still an outstanding interest to most people; as a thing of beauty when fully developed, they are well deserved subjects of admiration. When it is learned that they are merely hardy annuals, existing only for a single season completely disappearing every year only to promptly reappear, and then, in certain circumstances in an improved and enlarged form, admiration is exchanged for wonderment."

– A.I. McConnochie
Deer Forest Life, 1932

About the Author

Joe Shead (and yes, it's pronounced "shed") enjoys an outdoor life. In autumn he struggles to split his time between chasing deer and upholding the legacy of the gentleman waterfowler. His winters are devoted to ice-fishing, and late spring and summer finds him on the water almost every day, casting for largemouth bass, walleyes, northern pike and muskies (except for the excruciatingly painful year when he was trapped inside putting the finishing touches on this book while the fish were practically begging to be caught). However, his spring fishing time suffered severely the moment he found his first shed – a 4-point whitetail antler – and he's been hooked on shed hunting ever since.

Professionally, Joe is the managing editor of *Deer & Deer Hunting* magazine, where he is constantly absorbed in all things deer. His career benefits his hobbies of deer hunting and shed hunting, and vice versa. He enjoys the constant influx of knowledge of white-tailed deer he gains through reading and editing deer-hunting writing, communicating with deer hunters and biologists and through his time roaming the spring and autumn woods.

A Wisconsin native and resident all his life, Joe feels blessed to live in a state known for its great hunting, fishing and conservation leadership. He enjoys reading, writing, swimming, canoeing, carving duck decoys and scheming up new outdoor adventures when he can't be on the lakes or in the tamarack swamps.

Acknowledgements

I am extremely grateful to all those who helped me write this book, both directly and indirectly. I've got to start with Deb Salzer, who did a great job designing the book. She really made this whole thing possible, from designing to assisting with photos to staying up until all hours of the night to finish the book. She also slogged around through deep snow and wet swamps en route to finding her first antler, and would have found more if she just would have walked on the other side of me a few times. Thanks Deb!

I am forever indebted to Nick Morehouse, who not only got me hooked on shed hunting, but has taught me much about the pastime, as well as the natural beauty of the spring woods. Thanks to my brother Jack for his help with the photography and for being in the woods with me the day I found my first shed antler. Thanks to my brother Jim for his technical computer expertise. Thanks also to my parents, Jerry and Jeanne, for always asking, "How's that book coming?" – even in the middle of summer when shed hunting was the furthest thing from my mind – and for encouragement along the way.

Thank you to landowners George Piechowski and Dale Smith for allowing me to roam their land (especially George, on whose land I killed my first buck and found my first shed).

Thanks also to my friends and hunting partners Andy Lecker, Andy Chikowski, Jen Bybee and Ryan Bybee for their relentless photo-modeling efforts and editing skills. Thanks also for putting up with my nonstop talk about antlers and for being good sports about my deer camp shenanigans.

I'd also like to thank several sources of great shed-hunting information, including Doug and Tammy Coleman, Johnray Vance, the North American Shed Hunting Club and its members, the Iowa Whitetails Web site, Mike Lindquist of Minnesota Bucks and Tracy Bowling of Ventosa Kennel. And special thanks to Bentley Coben for taking me to his best shed-hunting spots and showing me what Canadian shed hunting is all about, and to Dianne Coben for her incredible home cooking, which kept me going all day, even after walking for 10 hours. Also, thank you Ron "Timbershadow" Strauss for your shed-hunting advice and enthusiasm for shed hunting and the white-tailed deer.

I'm also grateful to my sources of scientific information, including John Ozoga, Drs. George and Anthony Bubenik, Dr. Richard Goss, Charles Alsheimer, Dr. Leonard Lee Rue III, North Country Whitetails and the National Podiatric Medical Association.

A special thanks to *Deer & Deer Hunting* Editor Dan Schmidt for his constant enthusiasm for our shed finds, his strong knowledge of deer behavior and his ability to make work fun even during our busy times in summer.

Thanks also go out to Hugh McAloon, Brad Rucks, Jim Schlender, Paul Wait, Jacob Edson, Andrew Johnson, Brian Lovett, George Cuhaj, Duayne Kett, Donna and Jeffrey "Shooter" Bybee, Ben Kramlich and Signature Press.

And lastly, and most importantly, thanks to my Heavenly Father and my savior Jesus Christ, whom I remember to thank *almost* every time I'm fortunate enough to pick up a shed antler. Thank You for the ability to write this book, the courage to see it through and the time I enjoy in Your wonderful Creation.

Introduction

A lot of books about deer antlers start out by saying, "Antlers have fascinated man for centuries." If you're reading this book, you've probably already figured that much out, so I'll spare you the caveman stories.

The truth is, whatever fascination people have for antlers, either now or centuries ago, it is a justifiable one. Antlers are the fastest-growing tissue in the animal world – faster growing than even cancer cells. Plus, no other mammalian tissue falls off and regrows. Certain animal species, such as lobsters or newts, can regrow body parts. However, that ability is almost unheard of among mammals. There have been instances in which children have regrown missing digits, but these acts of regeneration are never fully complete and are apparently limited to youths, as adults have never been known to regrow fingers or toes. Male deer, on the other hand, are not only designed to regrow new antlers each year, but successive racks are typically even larger than the previous ones.

Antlers are mysterious, too. Why do deer grow antlers that fall off and regrow each year, while other animals, such as sheep, continue growing horns throughout their lives? And what's the difference between antlers and horns? Do antlers serve advantages over horns, or vice versa? What purposes do antlers serve?

Scientists have unraveled some of these mysteries, and others we'll never know. But this fascination with antlers is what drives us to want to learn more about them, to study them and even to search for them in woods and fields each spring. That last item is my focus in this book. It's my intent to not only "shed" some light on the mystery of antlers, but more importantly, to help you find more shed white-tailed deer antlers.

But why would anyone want to look for shed antlers? Well, why do writers put a pen to paper, or why do artists feel compelled to make that first brush stroke on canvas? I suppose it's because these folks simply feel the urge within to do so. The same could be said for shed hunters, but there are other reasons as well.

One common reason for shed seeking is deer hunters want to know how many bucks survived the deer season on their hunting grounds, but not all shed-hunting ventures are purely linked to deer hunting. Some seek antlers to make crafts for fun, decoration or profit. Others pick up antlers simply for their natural beauty. And there are those souls who see shed hunting simply as a good excuse to get outside after a long winter of being cooped up indoors and spend some time with family and friends. Whatever your reason for antler collecting, take comfort in the fact that you are not alone in your pursuit. In fact, many people who taste a bit of success afield experience something that borders on an obsession with shed hunting. After you find your first nice antler and go several days without finding the match, you'll soon see why.

I apologize if this book turns otherwise normal citizens into shed-seeking addicts who lie abed at night, wondering just where the matches to their shed antlers may be. In any case, I hope you'll find it a useful guide that helps you find more antlers and enjoy your time outdoors.

Why Search for Antlers?

Up until my college days, I'd been only the most casual of antler hunters, and it showed when browsing through my collection of zero (0) sheds. But one day when I got home from work, my roommate, Nick Morehouse, showed me three antlers he'd found that day while hiking, reinforcing the notion that shed hunting is far more productive than working. I'd always loved both hunting deer and watching them, and, like most people who are interested in deer, I liked deer antlers.

After seeing Nick's newfound antlers, and turning them over and over in my hands, I was salivating like one of Pavlov's dogs at dinnertime. This shed hunting was something I had to get into! When my brother Jack found two sheds while turkey hunting later that spring, it only fueled my desire to find an antler. Finally, on the last day of Jack's turkey season, he and I scoured the woods for sheds, and I finally found my first antler: a 4-point right side. It was an experience I'll never forget.

Today, I love antlers. I like to look at them, ponder how they grew and compare them with other antlers. I like the glossy look of a fresh shed, the twisting curve of a main beam and the heft of a new find in hand. It may sound crazy, but I know I'm not alone. Thousands of people share the same appreciation for antlers. Maybe it's the fact that each antler is unique, or the fact that when we hold an antler, we are holding a part of an animal that may be still alive. Every antler is a precious find for shed hunters. No matter how many sheds we find, each one has a story involving scouting, dumb luck or perseverance … and a special connection to a buck who may be still out there, waiting to tell another story in bone.

But aside from simply loving antlers, other things drive people to walk for hours on end for seemingly little or no gain. Shed hunting is an excuse to get outside after a long winter, when people like me, who have been sitting around a little too much all season, need it most. I have trouble sticking to a rigid exercise program, but I have no trouble going shed hunting, and I get great exercise, whether I'm on snowshoes early in the year or on foot later on. But of course I don't see it as exercise; to me, it's a labor of love.

Shed hunting also gives deer hunters great insight into what's going on in the whitetail's world. I can say without reservation that I've learned more about deer from shed hunting than from books and magazines or spending time deer hunting. Obviously, finding an antler is a good indication that a buck survived the winter. Shed hunting teaches you how deer travel, and areas that they not only prefer, but also those they avoid. If you live in an area with snow cover, you'll have a perfect medium to study tracks and deer movement through the woods while you search for antlers. Looking for sheds also gives you time to ponder what's going on in the deer woods, and when you do this and start asking questions about what you're observing, you start to learn things. All too often when we're deer hunting, we haven't the time to study what's happening as we hustle to our stands. Plus, worrying about controlling your odor and scaring deer is a nonfactor to the shed hunter, because deer will have months to return to their normal routine after you tramp through their territory.

Another enjoyable aspect of spending time in the woods looking for antlers is observing all the other things around you. It's refreshing to watch birds return and animals come out of hibernation on a 60-degree April day as the snow recedes and reveals hidden antlers. Taking in the fresh air makes you feel alive and I can think of no better way to spend a spring weekend, either alone or with friends and family. That's part of the real beauty of shed hunting. Unlike during deer season, when a squirming child could spook a deer, shed hunting is a great activity for you and your whole family. Searching for antlers lets you spend quality time with your friends and family and helps children take an interest in the outdoors at an early age. Children who tag along on shed hunts at a young age may be thoroughly interested in deer and deer hunting well before they're legally able to tote a gun. Plus, the outdoors is a great classroom for young and old alike. And, the more eyes in the woods, the better the odds of finding antlers.

Aside from all these great benefits of shedding, there's another reason why shed hunting is so popular: you can discover some truly huge whitetails. As deer hunters know, whitetails are wary creatures, especially large, mature deer. In fact, if you look at the Boone and Crocket Club record book, which is one of the most respected record-keeping organizations for big-game animals, you'll notice that the No. 1 and No. 2 nontypical bucks, which scored $333^{7}/8$ inches and $328^{2}/8$ inches, respectively, were both found dead. These deer survived for years without ever succumbing to a hunter's arrow or bullet, dropping sheds each year. In fact, whitetail sheds have been found that would certainly rival, and may actually exceed the racks of current world records. Of course, we won't know their exact score because a rack's inside spread is taken into account for scoring, and it's impossible to get an exact measurement when the antlers are detached from the skull. However, the North American Shed Hunters Club has established a way to recognize trophy-sized shed antlers as well. The NASHC record book, *Shed Antler Records of North American Big Game*, records record-sized shed antlers instead of whole racks.

Whether you're looking for exercise, time outside or antlers for a craft project, shed hunting is a great way to get outside and enjoy the outdoors.

Before You Begin

This book is designed to help you find more shed white-tailed deer antlers. However, before you read it, get inspired to find sheds and rush out the door expecting to find antlers with your newfound shed-hunting knowledge, let me offer some disclaimers.

First off, before you search for sheds anywhere, you should check with your state and local natural resources agency to make sure shed hunting is legal in your area. To the best of my knowledge, Ohio is the only state where shed hunting is not permitted. Nonresidents are also not allowed to collect shed antlers in Manitoba. I am not aware of any other states or provinces where collecting shed antlers is prohibited, but some states and provinces may restrict border crossings and things of that nature. Some specific areas may have shed-hunting restrictions. For example, state parks, wildlife refuges and some Canadian Crown lands may be off-limits to shed hunting. Shed hunting is also prohibited on public hunting lands in Illinois. Some western states have even toyed with the idea of putting a season on shed hunting to keep people from bothering winter-stressed animals before the snow melts, but to my knowledge no such laws have been enacted so far. Crossing the U.S./Canadian border with shed antlers is also regulated, but more about that in Chapter 6. As a safety precaution, you should always check with local law enforcement on rules and regulations of antler possession before heading out.

Despite the fact that I'm authoring the first book on shed hunting, I don't claim to be a shed-hunting expert. In fact, I know of and have met many folks who find more antlers in a single season than I could find in several years of shed hunting. However, I do believe my knowledge can be helpful to both beginner and veteran shed hunters alike, and that using the tips provided in this book, you can find sheds in any geographic region where whitetails are found. After all, deer must eat, travel and bed wherever they live, and they do so in a similar manner. Taking the path of least resistance and bedding to take advantage of sunny winter weather are universal whitetail behaviors. However, be aware that each geographic area has its own nuances that affect deer behavior.

For example, shed hunting in the mountainous West will require different methods than shed hunting in the Chicago suburbs or Kansas CRP fields. Deer in each of these areas have different bedding and feeding habits. The best way to learn what deer in your area feed on and where they bed is to get into the field and study deer behavior.

Also, weather in a particular geographic region can dictate deer movements and, in effect, the presence or absence of sheds. You may walk several miles in the Upper Peninsula of Michigan in winter without cutting a deer track. That's because deer may travel miles each fall to reach ancestral yarding areas where they can find food and shelter to keep them alive through cold, snowy winters. Likewise, deer in regions that receive deep snow may actually move closer to towns in winter. Here, they often find abundant food in the form of backyard shrubs, as well as food placed in feeders by people who love to watch deer. Travel is also easier for deer in towns because of plowed roads and shoveled sidewalks. Deer can also escape predators such as wolves, which dare not venture into town. But unless you know these little nuances of your particular shedding areas, you may be wasting your time.

I encourage you to read this book, learn from it, and then spend as much time as possible in your local shedding grounds to see how the information in this book pertains to your specific area. I suspect convincing most shed hunters to get afield more often won't be too hard. Good luck!

1
The Science of Antlers:
Pride Goeth Before the Fall

ntlers are a most unusual appendage. They are made of true bone, but strangely, they are the only bones known to grow outside of an animal's body. What is their purpose, and how do they form? We'll probably never know the real reason deer grow antlers, although many scientists have put forth compelling theories. Due to their bifurcated, or branched, structure, it has been suggested that antlers were developed specifically for fighting, as the tines of opposing bucks engaged in battle would "catch," preventing bodily injury to the combatants. Certainly bucks use their antlers for fighting, and they do so quite effectively, but antlers serve other purposes. In fact, the very sight of a large set of antlers is enough to drive off an inferior buck before a skirmish ever begins. Antlers are secondary sex characteristics, and as such, a large set of antlers is a true advertisement of a buck's health and vigor. It takes approximately four years for a buck to reach its maximum body size. Once body growth is complete,

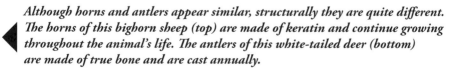

Although horns and antlers appear similar, structurally they are quite different. The horns of this bighorn sheep (top) are made of keratin and continue growing throughout the animal's life. The antlers of this white-tailed deer (bottom) are made of true bone and are cast annually.

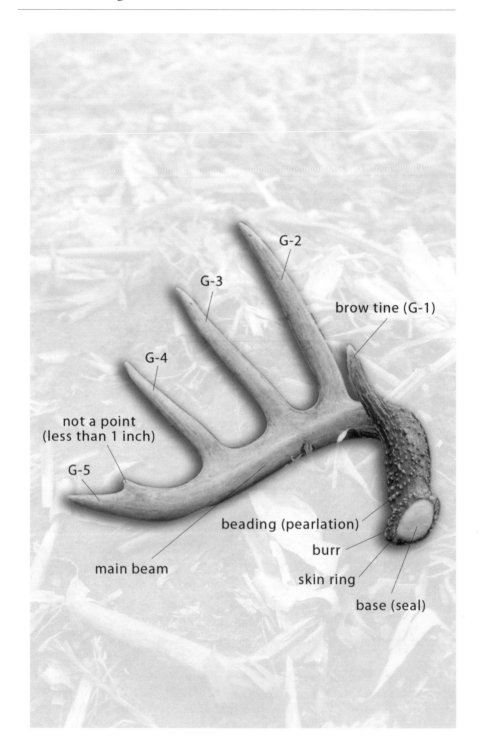

G-2

G-3

brow tine (G-1)

G-4

not a point
(less than 1 inch)

G-5

beading (pearlation)

burr

main beam

skin ring

base (seal)

a buck can dedicate more energy to antler growth. Typically, peak antler growth doesn't occur until a buck is 6 to 8 years old, or older. Therefore, a large rack indicates maturity, which serves to drive away smaller bucks during the rut, and is particularly attractive to does.

Horns in other animals serve the same basic functions as antlers, such as fighting and display. However, structurally, horns and antlers are very different. Horns consist of a bony core, covered in keratin; the same substance your fingernails are made of. Horns grow from the base, and continue growing throughout the life of the animal. Antlers, however, are made of bone. They grow from the tip, not from the base as horns do. After only about four months of growth, they calcify. Eight to 12 months after initial growth, antlers are shed, and soon after, new antlers develop. The reason antlers are replaced each year is uncertain. It has been proposed that because they are fragile and frequently break in combat, antlers are replaced in order so that bucks may grow a new rack devoid of structural damage each year. Another theory suggests that because bucks expend so much energy chasing does during the rut, and frequently lose a great deal of their body weight doing so, the presence of antlers during a harsh winter following a rigorous breeding season would readily advertise a buck's gender to predators looking to prey upon a weakened individual. Therefore, shedding their antlers helps bucks blend in with the rest of the herd. Theories abound trying to explain the reason for the annual shedding process, but despite our best theories, the true reason why bucks grow antlers remains a mystery.

Antler Growth

As soon as they're born, it's possible to distinguish male fawns from females merely by studying their heads. That's because already, dark swirls of hair have formed at the site of future antler growth: the pedicels.

The pedicels, located on top of a buck's head, just behind and above the eyes, are the source of antler growth. Whereas a buck's skull is composed mostly of compact plates, the pedicel is the exception. It is composed of spongy bone. It is literally the lifeblood and the sole connection between antlers and the rest of a buck's body.

Although well-nourished buck fawns may grow "infant antlers" measuring ½ inch or shorter when they are about 6 or 7 months old (which they also shed), most bucks – 90 percent or more – do not begin growing antlers until they are about 11 months old.

The pedicels, as seen on this skull from a buck that cast its antlers before it died, are located just above the eyes. These areas of spongy bone are the lifeblood and sole connections between antlers and the rest of a buck's body.

In the spring, when they are nearly a year old, bucks begin experiencing hormonal changes. As day length and sun intensity increase, the pineal gland, which is sensitive to changes in the amount of daylight, produces less melatonin. In winter, when days are shorter, melatonin prevents the pituitary gland from secreting gonadotrophins, which are hormones that stimulate the gonads. However, with less melatonin to suppress sexual hormones, hormones such as testosterone begin increasing. Because antlers are secondary sex characteristics and their development is linked to sex hormones, antler production also begins. It's important to note that although they are increasing, these hormone levels are still low, and bucks will remain infertile until about the time they rub off their velvet.

Antler growth, prompted by this slight increase in testosterone levels, starts slowly. First, antler buds form on the pedicel. Gradually, minerals flow to the newly emerging antlers, and are laid down as soft, spongy bone. Antlers are made mostly of calcium and phosphorus – essentially the same materials as other bones. These minerals are taken into the body from the food deer eat, and stored in the skeleton. When antler growth begins, these minerals are pulled from within a buck's existing skeletal structure and carried to the antlers. This exerts a

Growing antlers are covered with a material called velvet. Velvet antlers are the fastest-growing tissues in the animal kingdom.

tremendous physical drain on the body, thus, it's imperative that deer have a high-protein diet. Fortunately, antler growth coincides with the emergence of lush spring vegetation, which provides a smorgasbord for deer looking to not only recover from a long winter, but also prepare for fawning or antler growth.

Wrapped in Velvet

The antlers we observe in late spring and summer are quite different in appearance from the antlers we see in fall or winter. They are covered by a highly expandable hair-like material called "velvet," so named because these hairs give the growing antlers a velvety appearance. These hairs, as well as the large network of associated nerves, serve an important function. These highly sensitive sensory devices detect objects such as branches or brush and help bucks avoid damage to their antlers, which are extremely delicate in this stage. An injury to an antler while in velvet will severely deform it, certainly in the current growing season, and depending on the severity of the injury, perhaps in successive years.

Even though a buck may not be able to see its antlers, this nerve network gives him a good idea as to their height and width. This phenomenon is known as a "kinesthetic sense," and will remain with the buck as long as he carries his

Velvet's hair-like protrusions are sensory devices that warn bucks when they contact objects. Velvet antlers are very fragile and subject to damage.

antlers. Just as humans have no trouble anticipating how far to bend down as we sit, even though we can't see our backside, this same sense applies to bucks and their antlers. This perceptive ability helps bucks navigate quickly through dense cover without snagging their antlers.

In addition to the vast amount of nerves they contain, velvet antlers are also highly vascularized. In fact, so great is the volume of blood flowing through velvet antlers that they feel warm to the touch. A rich blood supply is necessary to support the tremendous growth rate of antlers, and blood flows through both internal blood vessels flowing through the pedicel, as well as blood vessels within the velvet. The latter frequently create channels that are still visible on the hardened antlers after the velvet is rubbed off.

Antlers grow proximally from the tip outward, meaning the main beams and brow tines grow before the distal tines (the G-2s, G-3s, etc.). As spring gives way to summer, antler growth speeds up, induced by rapidly rising testosterone levels. During peak growth, a white-tailed buck's antlers may grow ½ inch per day.

A few weeks before antler growth is complete, the outermost layer (under the velvet) begins to harden, influenced once again by rising testosterone levels, as the soft, spongy tissue mineralizes. Gradually, the mineralization process moves both inward and upward, starting near the base of the antler. Blood flow is constricted as the antler calcifies and becomes more dense. As blood flow within the antler is diminished, blood vessels within the velvet provide most of the nourishment. Eventually, however, blood vessels within the velvet also constrict, and the velvet dies and dries out, and so, too, dies the antler.

When the velvet dies, it begins to peel lengthwise. Bucks rub their hardened antlers on trees and other objects to help peel away the velvet. This can be a bloody ordeal, as typically blood still remains within the velvet. Bucks frequently consume these protein-rich bloody velvet shards upon removal, revealing hard, white (albeit blood-stained) antlers. It can take anywhere from a few hours to a few weeks for bucks to completely remove their velvet, dependent largely on the amount of experience a buck has with the process, and also the presence of such features as drop tines, which are difficult for bucks to rub against trees because of their odd configuration.

Even after the velvet is rubbed off, blood may still trickle within the antler. The innermost areas of the antler in particular remain somewhat porous before antler growth is finalized. In most cases, however, the antler is converted to solid bone within a few days of velvet removal, more than doubling its previous density, and residual blood flow is cut off completely.

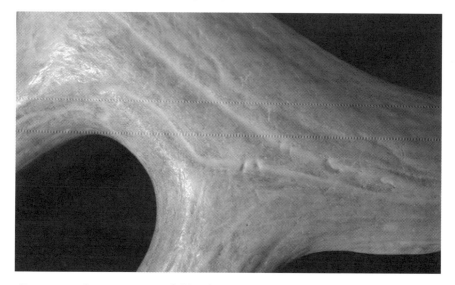

Growing antlers require a rich blood supply. After bucks rub off velvet, blood vessels that nourished the developing antler may still be evident.

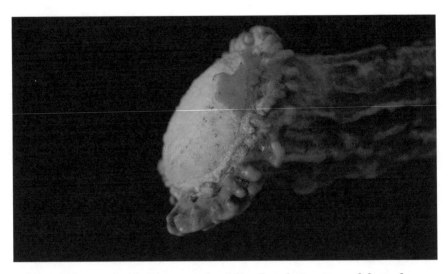

When testosterone levels drop, osteoclasts found at the juncture of the antler and pedicel reabsorb calcium from antlers. The reabsorption process creates pits and spicules, which give the base of a shed antler its rough texture. Eventually the tiny spicules are the only connection holding the antler in place. When they break, the antler drops.

Hardened antlers consist of an outer sheath of compact bone with a slightly spongier core. This softer core helps absorb the clash of antlers when bucks fight. However, in winter, antlers grow increasingly brittle, and they begin to dry out before they are cast.

The Shedding Process

Antler casting plays a significant role in a buck's life. The loss of his antlers immediately affects his social status in the herd. However, the process of shedding itself is amazingly fast and simple. It's been noted that you could literally drag a buck by its antlers one day, and they would fall off under their own weight the next.

Decreasing light levels, and in turn, decreasing testosterone levels, trigger shedding. As light levels decrease in winter, the pituitary gland, which controls hormone levels, also diminishes activity. As a result, testosterone levels decline, along with semen production.

As testosterone levels drop, cells called "osteoclasts," which are found at the juncture of the antler and pedicel, begin to reabsorb calcium from the antlers. As they do so, they create a series of pits and spicules that separate the antler from the pedicel. This is what gives the base of a cast antler its rough texture. As the reabsorption process continues, calcium is pulled ever more from the antlers, leaving fragile spicules as the sole attachment between the antler and pedicel. When these spicules break, the antler falls off.

With the antler gone, the bare, bloody pedicel is left exposed. The blood dries and scabs over in just a few days. Soon, skin begins growing over the pedicel, and when the pedicel is completely covered, the scab falls off. The skin will develop into velvet, and the antler cycle begins anew.

Timing of the Shedding Process

In order to find sheds, it's important to first determine a buck's location, and his reason for being there, at the time he casts his antlers. Because shedding can occur anytime from late November to early May in most areas of North America (bucks may shed at any time in Central and South America where the seasons are less defined), it's important to consider a buck's habits and habitats from winter to spring.

The exact time a buck casts his antlers is determined by several factors. Physical condition is a major consideration. The rut is a strenuous time for bucks, and seeking and tending estrous does wears them down. In northern areas, after the rut, bucks have only a short time to gorge themselves on available food and attempt to replenish fat reserves before deep snow makes acquiring food more difficult. Because mature bucks compete with other bucks and chase does so intensely, they are more likely to be worn out from the rut. Mature bucks also usually rank higher in the herd's social pecking order. But maintaining dominance is also physically demanding. When a buck drops his antlers, his dominance level immediately drops. Therefore, given their tendencies for greater physical exhaustion during the rut, and the high cost of maintaining large antlers, and in effect, high social rank, mature bucks sometimes drop their antlers first.

However, other factors come into play. Bucks that are better nourished usually carry their antlers longer. This is somewhat linked to how much of a toll the rut takes on a given buck, as a rut-weary buck will lose 20 to 25 percent of its body weight during the strenuous mating period. It would stand to reason, then, that bucks living where the deer population has exceeded the land's carrying capacity would shed earlier, due to an inordinate food supply.

Conversely, bucks living on range at or below carrying capacity should be better nourished and should carry their antlers longer. The same applies to deer that are supplementally fed in winter, either as a wildlife-management practice or simply in backyard feeders.

Latitude also affects antler casting. In Canada and the United States, deer physiology is linked to the seasons. Deer breed in the fall in order that does may drop their fawns in the spring, when food is abundant and at peak nutrition levels. This also gives fawns a long growing season, letting them put on critical body mass and fat reserves before winter. The same happens with antlers. Bucks begin growing their antlers in spring so they will be fully developed for use in combat and in attracting does during the breeding season. However, whitetail range isn't limited to the United States and Canada. The range of this adaptable deer extends south through Central America, and into South America, all the way to Peru. In more southern locations, where the change in seasons is barely noticeable, the timing of breeding, and therefore antler growth, isn't as crucial. In fact, in more southern climes, bucks may carry hardened antlers, velvet antlers or no antlers at the same time within the same deer herd! However, it stands to reason that the farther north you travel, the shorter the window in which breeding (and antler growth) can take place. Therefore, bucks in the north tend to shed earlier than those in the south.

In conjunction with latitude, weather affects antler drop. Harsh winters with deep snow and cold temperatures make finding food and simply surviving difficult. The harsher the winter, the more stress deer experience, and the earlier they shed. In harsh winters when deer concentrate on the best – and sometimes only – available food sources, bucks will tend to drop their antlers earlier and in more concentrated locations. In contrast, in areas where winter weather is milder and food more abundant, bucks will retain their antlers longer. Also, during mild winters, or in places where weather is less severe, deer can find food in many places, so they roam freely and drop their antlers on a more scattered basis.

Another interesting facet of antler drop is that individual deer tend to cast their antlers on nearly the same day each year. An individual buck will consistently shed within a few days of the same date each year. However, one thing that has gone largely unexplained is the synchronization of the shedding of both antlers. Sometimes both antlers fall off at the same time. Often this is caused by an action such as rubbing, jumping or feeding that knocks off the antlers. But more often than not, there is a lag between the fall of the first and second antler. Sometimes the second antler falls seconds later, mere feet from the first. More commonly, however, for reasons unexplained, the second antler lingers for a while. It usually falls off within three days of the first, but it's not unheard of for a buck to carry an antler a month or more after the first one falls off. Why this happens is baffling. If shedding is caused by reduced testosterone levels, it would seem logical that both antlers would fall off at the same time. Some theorize that the lag time between the shedding of the first and second antler may be due to social or psychological stress on the buck. At any rate, this phenomenon is simply another mystery waiting for science to "shed" some light on it.

Antler casting isn't determined by one trigger. A buck's health, stress level, dominance ranking and geographical location all influence his shedding date(s). Because of this, it's impossible to make broad, sweeping generalizations, like saying larger bucks shed first, or spike bucks shed first. Unfortunately for shed seekers looking to time it just right, antler drop varies from herd to herd and from individual to individual.

2
Find the Bucks First:
Location, Location, Location

Rather than walking blindly into the woods, it's wise to learn about the haunts and habits of deer in your area before you begin shed hunting. In order to find antlers with any consistency, we must understand a buck's location in winter and early spring.

After the chaos of the rut ends, for the most part, bucks separate from does and fawns. Most bucks separate from their mothers anywhere from about age 1 to 1½. Usually by their second fall (at about age 16 to 19 months), most bucks have dispersed from their natal range, established new home ranges and have done their best to fit into the fraternal hierarchy of other bucks. Thus, young bucks and older bucks will generally occupy the same territory, apart from does and fawns. Therefore, when shed hunting, you should avoid areas with obvious doe and fawn sign (such as small beds associated with larger beds) and seek buck sign (rub concentrations, antler imprints in snow, etc.). The only exception would be hot food sources, which will attract deer of both genders.

Before you can find shed antlers, you have to locate a buck's winter haunts. Sign such as rubs, beds, tracks and droppings can point you in the right direction.

Although some breeding still occurs in December, January and even later in the South, (and if a buck is breeding, his testosterone levels are probably too high for casting anyway) a buck's primary activities during winter are eating and resting. Therefore, we can concentrate our search on three main areas: bedding areas, feeding areas and the trails that link the two. However, a buck could drop his antlers anywhere on any given day. You may have identified a given buck's preferred food source, found his bedding area and discovered the connecting trail, but if a prowling coyote one day bumps him from his bed and he drops his antlers on a random stroll out of his preferred habitat, all your scouting is for naught. That being said, finding sheds, more than anything, is a percentage game. No matter how well you've patterned deer in your area, you'll never find all the sheds. In fact, even the best shed hunters, who are searching for antlers from a specific buck that they've seen many times, don't always find what they're looking for. You'll want to identify and search the most productive trails, bedding areas and feeding areas and try to eliminate unproductive real estate. Let's identify these three areas.

I usually begin my search for antlers each year in bedding areas for a few simple reasons. My shedding grounds are covered by snow in winter. It's quite easy to identify bedding areas in the snow, due to the readily visible beds, tracks and droppings. Because deer frequently bed in sunny, sheltered areas where the snow depth is reduced, there's a greater chance that antlers will be visible in bedding areas, even when heavy snow blankets most of the woods, so my search begins there when shedding fever sets in each year.

It's usually easier to find antlers in feeding areas and on trails after the snow melts, and when it does, I hit agricultural fields next. Deer spend a relatively large amount of time feeding in winter, plus, the physical action of eating puts a buck's antlers in contact with branches, cornstalks and the ground, which may serve to remove them.

Trails are my last resort. I search them when things begin greening up in the spring. Then I don't have to worry about scanning a thick, green jungle for antlers because they should be right at my feet. Odds are most antlers will be cast in bedding or feeding areas, and many people spend their time searching these areas instead of trails. But despite the fact that bucks spend less time walking than they do bedding and feeding, deer trails have been good to me, and I do find a lot of antlers on them. Just as with feeding, motion often plays a part in antler casting when deer use trails, and often to a much greater extent.

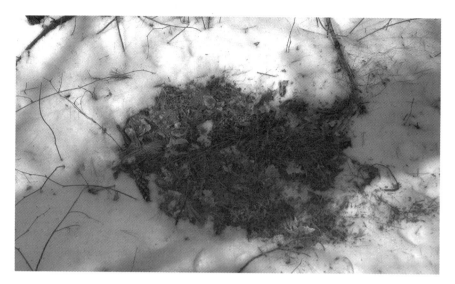

When shed hunting, avoid areas where large beds are surrounded by small beds, which would indicate a doe with fawns. A buck's body is larger than a doe of the same age. Also, a buck may bed in areas of less cover, but with better access to food sources, particularly on a southern exposure. Does often bed in thick cover.

Even though deer spend comparatively little time traveling during winter, the actions of ducking under branches, jumping over fences and squeezing through brush cause bucks to shed their antlers while walking quite frequently.

Bedding Areas

All deer, whether they live in the frozen extremes of Canada or the milder climates of the southern United States, go through biological changes to adjust to cold winter weather. Whether or not they must deal with below-freezing temperatures and deep snow, deer grow thicker winter coats and their metabolism slows in response to the onset of winter. In order to survive cold, snowy winters, bucks must conserve energy. As a result, they spend a great deal of time bedded. Bucks prefer to bed where they can minimize the effects of cold winter weather. For this reason, bedding areas typically consist of some type of dense cover, such as an evergreen forest or a briar thicket. In winter or early spring, bedding areas are easy to identify. Beds will appear as oval depressions in snow or leaf litter. Deer droppings will be plentiful after a winter's worth of accumulation. Plus, there will likely be numerous trails within the cover, with major ones leading to food sources.

The type of places deer will bed in winter depends on the severity of winter in the area and the type of cover available. If the winter is mild and without snow, deer may use the same basic summer and winter range. If the area is heavily wooded, deer may prefer some types of woody cover over others, but if there is little wooded cover, deer may bed in creek bottoms, wooded draws or marshes.

Another point to consider is after the rut, bucks separate from does and may reform old bachelor groups with other bucks. Thus, you're more likely to find bucks bedded together, rather than with does and fawns. Therefore, if you're finding doe and fawn sign, such as obvious fawn tracks, or small beds in close proximity to larger ones, it may be wise to keep searching until you find buck sign. On the same vein, once you've found a buck bedding area, search it hard. It's quite common to find multiple antlers from different deer in the same area, so when you know you're in buck territory, keep searching.

Typical Bedding Areas

As with most things pertaining to shed hunting, the exact locations where deer bed depend on geographic region. Here are some classic examples of bedding areas.

Deer droppings are good indicators of deer activity, especially in areas where a lack of snow makes beds and trails hard to see.

Evergreens along food sources are great places to find sheds. The trees block the wind and reduce snow depth, and deer need only rise from their beds to eat.

Thick stands of conifers make textbook bedding areas. The variety of tree matters little. Deer may utilize a naturally occurring cedar swamp, a five-year-old pine plantation or any type of coniferous cover. The main objective is shelter from predators and the cold. The dense assortment of limbs in evergreen forests blocks heat-robbing wind, and it also forms a heat-trapping canopy, making these dense stands just a few degrees warmer than the surrounding areas. Also, the thick branches on coniferous trees catch snowfall, if present, keeping it off the ground and making it easier for deer to travel. It may not seem like enough to make a difference, but if you've ever walked into such a stand of evergreens on a snowy winter day, you know that the deer are onto something. For these reasons, conifer stands are very appealing to deer in winter, and they are prime areas to search for sheds.

South-facing hillsides are another common bedding site. Here, deer aren't looking for thick cover. In fact, they're trying to be out of the cover, at least a little bit. These areas receive the most direct sunlight during the winter in the northern hemisphere. Not only does this sun feel good on a warm winter day, but it melts the snow here first. It's not unusual to find a south-facing slope devoid of snow, while the surrounding areas are still buried by a foot or more of the white stuff. Southern hillsides, like any other hillsides, also help deer see approaching predators, and, depending on the wind direction and time of day, help them smell predators as well. In fact, the southern exposure is a key to deer movement and bedding in any area, whether it's on a hill or flat land. In addition to southern hillsides, search the south edge of a woods first, particularly if that edge is along an agricultural field. Always keep direction in mind as you walk, and be sure to check the southern exposure of any type of cover deer may bed in or under, be it a vast forest or a lone pine in a field.

Thick, brushy areas are also good bets because not only do they provide bedding cover, but thick tangles of brush often serve to remove antlers. Tag alder, willows and red-osier dogwood are thick-growing species that hold deer in my area of the Midwest, but search whatever thickets are available in

Lone evergreens stand out from their surroundings and attract deer and other animals. Deer frequently bed under them.

your area. Once again, deer are looking for thick, protective cover that they can bed securely in. I once found an old, green antler with a drop tine on a trip to Alabama. I wasn't supposed to be shed hunting, but I squeezed in an hour of searching and came up with the find. I don't know what kind of thicket I was searching in, but it was thick and brushy. It looked like the perfect spot for a deer to bed, and apparently at least one buck agreed with my assessment.

One of my favorite places to search for deer beds and associated antlers is underneath evergreen trees, particularly lone pines among hardwoods or lone pines in the open. As mentioned, conifers catch the snow and block the wind. In snow country, trying to find sheds early in the calendar year can be frustrating because of deep snow. However, quite often, there will be little or no snow under big pines, particularly if they are in the open or have a southern exposure. I also believe deer are attracted to these trees when they are isolated or are the only conifers in a deciduous forest. I believe deer, and other animals, for that matter, relate to these "landmarks" the same way a fish relates to rocks, weeds or stumps. It's that odd piece of cover that attracts their attention. More often than not, you'll find deer beds or droppings under them, and if you're lucky, maybe you'll find an antler there too.

Creek bottoms often make excellent bedding areas. Cover along streams tends to be thick and nasty. In fact, in more wide-open areas, creek bottoms may provide the only suitable bedding areas. Muddy trails and tracks in the moist soil also help you pinpoint deer movement. Search creek bottoms hard whenever you find them.

Other isolated features, such as windfalls, also make good spots for deer to lie down. Windfalls block the wind and provide thick cover. Fallen trees may also still carry browse or mast that doubles as a food source.

And speaking of food, if you find a good bedding area in close proximity to a food source, so much the better. Deer, like all wild creatures, minimize their activity to conserve energy, particularly in winter. A good bedding area near a feeding area, such as a thick growth of pines along a cornfield, is especially attractive to deer.

Good bedding areas are where you find them. The more you understand the habitat in your particular area and how deer use it, the easier it will be for you to identify likely bedding areas. Watch for areas that provide cover, cut the wind and reduce the snow level and you're likely to find a bedding area.

Going Yard

In far northern areas that receive heavy snowfall, deer may make annual winter migrations to traditional deer yards. These yards consist of thick conifer swamps, ideally white cedar, but deer will also use hemlock, balsam fir and white and black spruce. Although the long journey to these areas, sometimes dozens of miles, would seem to be a major energy drain, the benefits of traditional yards obviously must be worth the costs.

A deer yard offers a few definite advantages. These swamps offer protection from the wind and reduced amounts of snow on the ground. Also, dozens of deer may concentrate in a single area, which helps to pack down trails in heavy snow, making navigation easier and lessening the chances of being preyed upon by predators.

In places such as the Upper Peninsula of Michigan, where snow is measured in feet instead of inches, deer commonly bed in white cedar swamps. White cedar not only provides bedding cover, but it is the only woody browse that provides deer with enough nutrition in winter to offset the energy expended to obtain it. Bucks will usually spend their time on the edges of thick swamps, where they have better access to food, but less thermal cover. Does tend to head for core areas where they are better sheltered from the elements.

Although yards provide both food and shelter, they have some serious drawbacks. With high deer concentrations and heavy snow accumulation, finding food is of major concern. Does may fight their own fawns for food, and once the lowest branches have been browsed, only the largest deer will be able to reach food higher up in the trees. Also, predation becomes easier, as wolves, bobcats and coyotes have an easier time catching concentrated, winter-weary deer in deep snow.

However, despite these serious drawbacks, the advantages of deer yards must outweigh the disadvantages, because deer have been using them, and surviving in them, for centuries. One word about ethics, however. Although deer will be highly concentrated in deer yards, making for good shed hunting, even in big-woods country where deer populations are relatively low, remember, these deer are pitted in a struggle for survival. Walking through deer yards during winter causes undue stress to these already weakened animals. If you're going to search deer yards, do so in spring when the snow is gone and deer can find food once again. The antlers will still be there.

Deer love corn, and cornfields are excellent places to shed hunt. However, the sheer size of cornfields and the color and shape similarities between cornstalks and antlers makes finding sheds difficult.

Feeding Areas

Winter is a trying time for whitetails. In areas where cold and deep snows are frequent, deer struggle to find enough food to stay alive. Deer don't hibernate, as some animals do, but their metabolism slows down in winter, and deer move and eat less than they do at other times of the year. This saves precious energy, which lowers the amount of food deer must eat in winter to survive. When deer aren't eating, they're usually resting. Deer may decrease their daily activity by 50 percent or more in winter, and even limit their feeding and movements to midday to reduce heat loss in extremely cold weather. All in all, a deer requires about 30 percent less food in winter than at other times of the year. However, in some areas, deer have a tough time even finding that much food, and it is quite normal for deer to burn some of their fat reserves and lose weight over the winter.

Deer eat a wide variety of foods in winter – even some that they eat at no other time of year – simply because finding food can be so difficult. In areas

Trees that fall naturally or as a result of logging practices provide young, tender browse for hungry deer. The trees also act as cover and double as bedding areas.

When food is in short supply, deer will do anything to get it. Here, deer have blazed heavy trails from a tamarack swamp to the corncribs in the barnyard.

where winter survival is a struggle, deer will eat nearly anything they can find – even tree bark, which has no real nutritional value – just to calm the rumbling in their stomachs.

Fortunately, in most areas, deer aren't that hard pressed to survive. In woodland areas, deer browse on white cedar, honeysuckle, red maple, creeping cedar, red osier dogwood and any number of browse species, depending on the region. When and where it's available, deer will feed on mast (such as acorns and apples) as well, pawing through deep snow if necessary to find it.

In agricultural areas, deer regularly feed on crops such as alfalfa, corn, soybeans, barley and others. In fact, deer sometimes boldly sneak right into the barnyard, where they help themselves to corn in corncribs and bales of hay.

Food plots can also be great sources of winter deer food. A variety of species attract deer in winter, including rye, rape, turnips and many other plantings. If plots stay green throughout the winter, they will be particularly appealing to deer.

Attracting deer to backyard feeders is also popular for wildlife enthusiasts. Deer are commonly fed corn in feeders, but won't stop at just grain once they're in a residential yard. In fact, whether they're invited in or not, deer frequently enter residential yards where they feed on birdseed, shrubs, apple trees and many other plants, often to the chagrin of homeowners.

South-facing hillsides, already mentioned as excellent bedding areas, double as feeding areas. The sun melts snow here first, exposing acorns, grasses, farm crops and other food sources, while the surrounding area remains buried by snow. Find a southern slope, and plan to spend extra time looking.

Pay attention to what's going on in the forests and fields around you. Spend some time outside, even if deer aren't shedding yet, so you can familiarize yourself with what they're feeding on. The results may surprise you. For instance, one year, probably around March, there was a major windstorm. A red maple blew down right behind my house. With spring only days away according to the calendar, the tree had already formed buds. The deer found that tree and ripped it to shreds. In just a few days you couldn't find a bud on it within a deer's reach. By the end of the week, the ground beneath the tree was absolutely covered with deer droppings. I never found a shed under that tree, but I was hopeful because I knew some deer were still carrying antlers.

Natural Browse

Despite the popularity of shed hunting near crop fields and food plots, it's important to remember that deer are browsers, and naturally occurring browse species make up a large portion of their diet, even when crops are available. For that reason, (and especially because crops aren't available in all areas) it's important to key in on what species of natural browse deer feed on in your area.

Weather, to some extent, dictates what deer eat in winter. If you live where winters are mild, deer will likely continue eating whatever browse species were available in fall. In areas where winters are more severe, deer may travel to areas like white cedar swamps or aspen groves with creeping cedar carpeting the ground to get at these evergreen browse species because 1. They provide nutrition and 2. Deer can get at them in winter. Deer aren't very particular about what they eat if they are struggling to survive. If they can get at a source of food, whether it's branches or bark, deer may eat it in winter. Deer will always strive to eat preferred species if they're available – they'll

Despite the presence of agricultural crops and food plots, deer feed extensively on natural browse. In Canada's plains region, creeping cedar attracts deer in winter, left. In the Midwest, deer often browse on red osier dogwood, right.

paw through a foot of snow to get at acorns in winter – but availability is often the limiting factor.

How do you know what deer are browsing on? Deer leave many clues as to what they've been feeding on, whether your area has easy-to-read snow on the ground or not. Look for tracks in snow or mud. At a highly preferred food source, such as an apple tree that carries fruit into the winter, deer tracks may cover the ground like divots on a golf ball. Other indications include nipped-off buds, dropped food (such as hemlock sprigs dropped under a hemlock tree) paw marks in the snow and concentrations of deer droppings. You can also identify what deer eat by noting where you observe deer or by following their tracks from known bedding areas. Also, be sure to make note of any trees that fall either naturally or as a result of logging. It doesn't take deer long to discover fallen trees, the branches of which are now at a height where deer can readily feed on them.

Some of the best places to find deer are areas where the same species provides both food and cover. White cedar trees, already mentioned, do the job in the North. In the South, Japanese honeysuckle fills the bill. Although the species isn't native to the United States, deer, as they so often do, have adapted to take advantage of it. The thick vines form great cover for deer, and the plant stays green all winter, providing great forage. In fact, while some people try to kill off the invasive plant, some deer managers fertilize it to provide better deer habitat and food. The plant can yield up to 1½ tons of forage per acre and provide 10 to 20 percent protein.

Staging Areas

Pay attention to where deer enter feeding areas. A short walk into the protective cover will usually reveal a staging area. Before deer enter open fields to feed at night, they often leave their bedding areas and lounge around in staging areas, which typically consist of brushy cover just back into the woods from feeding areas. Here, they mill about, waiting impatiently for the cover of darkness before entering a field to feed. Because deer are on the move in these areas and because of their brushy, antler-stripping makeup, staging areas can be prime shedding locales.

Trails

In addition to bedding and feeding areas, trails can also be good places to find sheds. They are readily visible, and they make it easy to determine where and how deer move through the woods. Although deer spend most of their time eating and resting in winter, and only a small amount of time using trails, activities such as jumping a fence, crossing a ditch, going through brush or passing under a low-hanging branch may help bucks shed antlers. Of course, sometimes antlers simply fall off as a deer walks from Point A to Point B. So, even though bedding and feeding areas are probably better prospects, spend time each spring walking deer trails, particularly after spring green-up, when visibility is reduced in forests and crop fields.

When covering a deer trail, don't fall into the trap of merely looking at your feet. When you're tracking a deer, you obviously have to look down to follow the deer's spoor, but you also have to look up ahead of you so you can spot the deer before it sees you. The same holds true for shed hunting along deer trails. You should be able to see any antlers lying on the trail in your peripheral

Male deer frequently shed while traveling along deer trails. Buck trails are usually less traveled than doe trails and are more direct.

vision. Spend the majority of your time scanning off to the sides of the trail so you can cover more ground as you walk. One trick to consider, if you're really trying to stack the shedding odds in your favor: avoid walking along trails in thick brush that's prone to snapping off. Instead, parallel the trail from a close distance, if possible. You want to leave every antler-grabbing limb intact so you can more easily locate sheds in the future. You might even manipulate branches over a deer trail to encourage shedding.

Identifying deer trails usually isn't a problem. Trails appear as a line of matted-down leaves in forests, a string of trampled grass in fields and deep ruts in snow. In fact, in snow country, trails from the previous fall will be revealed in the spring, perfectly intact, and trails used heavily during the winter will be readily identifiable.

Which trails should you search? I admit, there are days when I bounce from trail to trail on a whim, with no game plan or destination in mind. Taking up a trail is a good way to put on miles, and most of the time the antlers will be right at your feet. But not all trails are created equally. Bucks and does often travel on separate trails. If you learn which trails bucks frequent, you will increase your chances of finding sheds.

You've probably come across big, muddy trails that look like deer superhighways. In a lot of cases, they would probably be more appropriately named *doe* superhighways. Often, these major trails are frequented by does. There are exceptions, of course. If such a trail leads to a hot food source, both bucks and does may travel it, especially in the winter. Likewise, deer of both sexes will travel major trails when the terrain forces them to do so, such as when traversing a creek crossing or a saddle of land between two ridges. However, bucks often leave major trails to the does, while they take less-developed paths. These faint buck trails usually parallel doe trails, but they tend to lead through cover more often and skirt the edges of open areas. Bucks frequently travel in a more direct line than does, and they tend to cut corners, rather than making a square corner like a doe might. Finding rubs and scrapes along a trail is an excellent indication that bucks are using a particular runway, and rubs are always worth checking out to see if a buck has shed an antler while working over a tree.

Finding buck trails, as opposed to doe trails, takes scouting and woodsmanship. But one of the joys of shed hunting is the knowledge you gain about deer movements and behavior. Such information will help you become a much better shed hunter, deer hunter and woodsman.

STICKER POINT:

Hotspots and Cold Spells

Shedding areas, like deer-hunting areas, can have their ups and downs. One year you may find several sheds in a particular spot, only to blank the next.

That describes one of my favorite shedding areas perfectly. One year I found fully half of my sheds for the year on one parcel of land, and the following year I found only one old shed there. What happened? Something changed.

Anytime you find yourself in a similar position, you have to analyze the situation. What's different about the area now? Any number of things can change from year to year. Keep in mind that the change doesn't have to occur on the property you walk. It might be a mile or two away. At the landscape level, the area could be developed, crops could be rotated or forests could be cut. Consider social changes. Perhaps the area received increased hunting pressure, or poachers could have gone on a spree. Maybe new neighbors fed deer over the winter, which altered deer movements. Weather could also be a factor. Deer may change wintering areas in accordance with the severity of the winter weather.

Take a look at the big picture and adapt if possible. In my example, a neighboring landowner did an extensive timber cut in late winter, which I believe altered deer patterns. Slash from the cut provided deer with a fresh supply of browse and cover, and I didn't find a single fresh shed on one of my favorite spots.

Although shedding grounds can go cold, just remember, when they do, somewhere else things are heating up. Take a look around and try to cash in.

3
Equipment and Preparations

S hed hunting is a refreshingly simple activity that requires nothing more than a comfortable pair of hiking boots and a sharp pair of eyes. To tell you the truth, most days that's all I bring with me. But if you're planning a full day of hard-core antler seeking, here are a few things you might want to bring along.

Shed-Hunting Checklist

- **Water and food.** A full day of walking will wear you out, and you need to eat and drink to keep going. You don't have to go overboard here. Pack a simple bag lunch or bring some granola bars, bagels and apples.
- **Toilet paper.** Enough said.
- **Medicines.** Be sure to bring along any medications that you take regularly.
- **Compass.** When you're searching diligently, it's not hard to become disoriented. A compass can get you out of the woods, or back to a secret hotspot.

◀ *Shed hunting requires very little equipment. However, if you're spending all day in the field, a few essentials will get you through the day and back to the truck.*

- **Binoculars.** A small, but powerful pair of binoculars are nice to have. You can check out possible sheds from a good distance away, and check the heads of deer you kick up to see if they're still carrying antlers.
- **Boots.** The weather and terrain will dictate the footwear to wear. Early in the season warmth and traction might be the key on snowy terrain. In spring, rubber boots might be the ticket because of standing water following snowmelt. In open areas or dry woods, hiking boots should be fine. Whatever boots you wear, be sure they're broken in and capable of putting on a lot of miles without hurting your feet. (More on foot care later.)
- **Socks.** Socks are often overlooked. Get a pair that provide some cushion and that will keep your feet dry. Synthetic blends are best because they wick moisture away from your feet.
- **Clothing.** Clothing also depends on the weather. Keep in mind that you'll be walking, so you want something that will keep you warm, without overheating. Dress in layers so you can remove clothing if you get overheated. Clothing should be comfortable and allow maximum freedom of movement. You might also want to consider brush pants in thick, thorny areas or other specialized clothing suited to the areas you'll be walking.
- **Radio.** If you're searching with a friend, a radio comes in handy to keep in contact.
- **Topographic map.** A topographic map gives you a good overview of the area, and can show you such things as south-facing hillsides and low-lying swamps.
- **Camera.** People love taking "as they lay" photos of sheds. Bring a camera to capture the memory.
- **Rope.** You never know when you have to string up a bunch of sheds just to get them all out of the woods.
- **GPS unit.** A GPS unit could come in mighty handy in the woods. It can mark the places where you find antlers, and help you get back to your vehicle at the end of the day.
- **Cell phone.** In this day in age, everyone seems to be carrying a cell phone. It's never a bad idea to carry one when you're in the woods. All it takes is a twisted ankle a mile from the car to get you in trouble. Even if you do have a phone, it's still a good idea to let someone know where you're going and when you expect to return in case you lose reception.
- **Backpack.** A backpack will help you carry all this stuff, plus a pile of sheds.

Serious shed seekers employ a variety of footwear to help them find cast antlers during the changing weather conditions of winter and spring.

Foot Care

It's hard to think of a negative aspect of shed hunting in the spring woods, but if there is one, it's the fact that shed hunting can be rough on your feet. Think about it: you're walking for hours at a time, on uneven terrain, often in soupy spring conditions. That's a recipe for disaster on your feet. But of course, no shed hunters I know would let a little foot discomfort keep them out of the woods each spring. This section is designed to help you put on the miles in comfort.

The subject of foot care, as it pertains to shed hunting, can be a complex one. Ideally you'll be wearing a well-broken-in pair of comfortable hiking boots, but that's not always possible. It seems shed hunters will go just about anywhere if they know antlers are on the ground, and that means that in addition to the usual hiking boots, shed-seekers also wear snowshoes, heavy winter pac boots, knee-high rubber boots and even waders. These alternative boot styles obviously won't fit like a pair of good hiking boots, and each has its own particular demands.

For cold-weather walking, polypropylene liners with heavy wool socks will keep your feet warm and dry. However, make sure these heavy socks don't make your feet fit too snugly in your boots or your feet will get cold in a hurry. Rubber boots may be necessary in muddy fields or soggy swamps, but they can be hard on your feet. Treat any hot spots (areas that are forming blisters) immediately and change into clean, dry socks frequently.

Assuming you'll be wearing hiking boots for most of your outdoor forays, follow these guidelines for footwear selection. The most important "step" is obviously selecting a pair of boots that fits well; not too tight, not too loose. Get boots that have wiggle room in the toes, but minimal heel slip. The last thing you want is a boot rubbing on your heel all day. The heel and arch should offer plenty of support, but the toes should be flexible (both for walking and feeling any sheds you may step on). Breathable footwear made of leather or nylon is best, and you'd be wise to consider Gore-Tex material that keeps moisture out while still letting your feet breathe. Boots should fit well as soon as you buy them, but it's a good idea to break them in a bit before you do any serious shed hunting. A good pair of boots, if properly cared for, will serve you for years and can be worn for spring shed hunting, summer camping trips and fall upland bird and deer hunting. Socks are equally important. They cushion your feet, keep them warm in cold weather and when used properly, control moisture, which is the ultimate enemy of hikers. Your typical cotton socks are a poor choice for shed hunting because they quickly grow wet with sweat. This is bad for a few reasons. Wet socks promote bacterial growth that causes foot odor and athlete's foot. Wet feet also help form blisters and cause your feet to grow cold. Instead of cotton socks, consider wool or synthetic socks. Wool socks keep your feet warm, even when wet, but they can't wick moisture away from your feet like today's synthetic blends. For that reason, synthetic socks are your best choice. One good technique is to wear two pairs of socks: one snug-fitting, moisture-wicking liner sock inside a good wool or synthetic-blend sock. Wearing two pairs of socks greatly reduces the friction that causes blisters.

You might also consider orthotic inserts. They not only cushion your feet, but they can also keep your foot from sliding in your boots.

The American Podiatric Medical Association has identified some of the most common hiking-related foot ailments you're likely to experience, and has provided instructions to prevent and treat these uncomfortable and painful byproducts of shed hunting.

Blisters: Blisters are one of the most common foot problems for shed-seekers. These fluid-filled areas of raised skin are caused by friction from socks or improperly fitting shoes. Moisture also contributes to their formation. It follows, then, that blisters can be prevented by wearing properly fitting boots and synthetic socks that wick moisture away from the skin. When you first feel a "hot spot" forming on your foot, stop walking, take off your shoe and apply moleskin or a bandage and antibiotic ointment to reduce friction. To treat an existing blister, sterilize a needle by holding it in a flame, then poke small holes in the blister where it meets the skin to drain the fluid. Leave the skin intact, and apply antibiotic ointment and a bandage. If the area appears infected, see your doctor.

Athlete's foot: Athlete's foot, that familiar foe of the locker room, is no stranger to the shed hunter. This fungal infection of the skin is caused by excessive sweating or hiking in wet boots and socks. To prevent athlete's foot, wear waterproof, breathable boots and socks that wick moisture away from your feet. Using foot powders will also keep your feet dry and prevent athlete's foot from developing. If your feet get wet, put on clean, dry socks as soon as possible. Athlete's foot can be treated with over-the-counter anti-fungal creams.

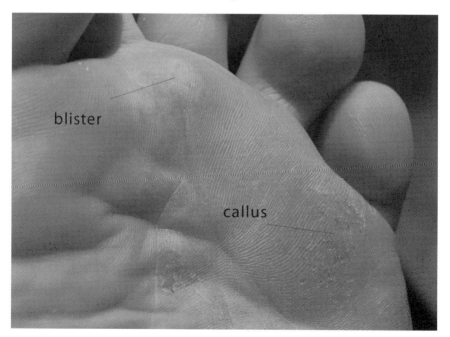

If you want to find antlers, take care of your feet. Foot ailments such as blisters (center) and calluses (right) will slow you down in the woods.

Ankle sprains: Ankle sprains are common when hiking in the uneven, obstacle-strewn terrain bucks call home. Sprained ankles are usually caused by stepping on an uneven surface such as a hidden log or hole, and they tend to happen without warning. Your best prevention is to wear high boots that offer ankle support. Depending on the severity, a sprained ankle may keep you out of the woods for a while. To treat an ankle sprain, the APMA recommends you remember RICE: Rest, Ice, Compression bandage (such as an Ace bandage) and Elevation.

Heel or arch pain: Heel or arch pain occurs when the fibrous band of tissue running from the heel through the arch of the foot becomes inflamed. This pain usually results from a lack of proper support for the foot, either from poorly constructed shoes or worn-out footwear. People who do a lot of hiking are especially prone to heel or arch pain. Pain in these areas can be avoided by wearing boots with proper support or wearing orthotic inserts. Gradually training for long hikes is also helpful. The pain can be treated by wearing boots with adequate support, resting, applying ice, using anti-inflammatories and stretching (particularly calf stretching).

Corns and calluses: Corns and calluses are thick layers of compacted, dead skin. They are caused by friction and pressure from skin rubbing against bony areas of the foot or your boot. To prevent corns and calluses, make sure your boots fit properly and consider orthotic inserts. Consult your doctor for help on removing them.

When you're done shed hunting for the day, inspect your feet for potential blisters, and treat as necessary. Clean and dry your feet to prevent athlete's foot and apply foot powder to your toes and moisturizing cream to the rest of your feet. If your feet are swollen, elevate them and apply ice. It's also wise to dry your boots if you plan on heading out again soon.

Ticks

One nice thing about shed hunting is that it usually takes place in early spring when mosquito numbers are low or nonexistent. However, it seems ticks emerge earlier every year, right in concurrence with prime shed hunting time. With today's concerns over contracting tick-borne diseases, such as Lyme disease, it's important to know how to deal with ticks.

Your first defense against ticks is to use an insect repellent containing 100 percent Deet or permethrin, which have been proven to repel ticks. In addition to applying insect repellents, you might also consider rolling your socks over your pant legs to keep ticks from reaching your legs. Wearing gaiters or even wrapping duct tape around the bottom of your pants legs serves the same purpose. Wear light-colored clothing when you shed hunt so ticks are more visible, and remove them as soon as you find them.

Ticks are the bane of spring shed seekers. They burrow into your skin and can even transmit diseases. Wear light-colored clothing and check for ticks when you get home from shed hunting.

When you get home from your shed-hunting outing, inspect your body for ticks and remove any of the blood-sucking insects immediately. Ticks that are crawling on you can simply be brushed off. The best way to remove ticks that have bitten you is to remove them with a tweezers. Grasp the tick firmly toward the head, and pull. A small piece of skin should remain in the tick's mouth. This is a visual indication that no mouth parts were left behind attached to your skin. If the mouth parts are left behind, try to remove them with the tweezers. Once the tick is removed, wash your skin with soap and water and apply anti-bacterial ointment.

Ticks are known to transmit several diseases, often dependent on your geographic region. One of the most common is Lyme disease, which is prevalent in the Northeast and Midwest where shed hunting is especially popular. A tick must be attached to you for about 24 hours before it can pass along Lyme disease. A telltale early warning sign that you've contracted Lyme disease is the formation of a circular red rash where the tick bite occurred. Later symptoms of the disease include flu-like symptoms. If you think you may have contracted Lyme disease, see your doctor immediately. Early detection and treatment by a physician helps your body combat the disease.

4
Seeking Fallen Bone

Yd ou can stumble on a shed antler just about anywhere. A big-city youth might have never seen a wild buck in his life, and then one day find a shed antler lying in the middle of a bike trail in a city park. On the contrary, a devout shed hunter may spend nine months of the year anxiously awaiting the return of late winter and a fresh crop of sheds. Then he might walk for eight hours, scouring every inch of farm-country real estate and come up empty. Shed hunting is a game of scouting, strategy and sometimes a lot of luck. There's never a guarantee that you'll find antlers on any given day, but the thought that they *are* out there keeps shed hunters going.

My first shed hunts were aimless walks through the woods. Oh sure, I'd follow deer trails and check out beds, but I might as well have been looking for a pot of gold at the end of the rainbow. But the more I searched, and the more I talked about shed hunting with other people, the more I began to learn about deer habits and shed hunting. With learning came a certain amount of understanding. "This buck jumped a fence here, jarring his body when he landed. So *that's* why this antler is laying here." After that came extrapolation. "If a buck lost an antler jumping over a fence, it would be a good idea to check for antlers at creek crossings, fallen logs and other places where a buck has to jump over an

Whitetails begin shedding as early as late November. Antlers can be hard to find when buried by snow, but the sooner you find them, the less chance they'll be gnawed on by rodents. Photo by Doug Coleman.

obstacle." I am always learning new things as I follow deer tracks and read deer sign in the woods. In fact, shed hunting has taught me more about deer and how to hunt them than any magazine or video ever could. It seems most days I come out of the woods with more questions about deer behavior than I started with. Some days I stumble upon a shed in an area where I never expected to find one. And every once in a while, I analyze deer movements and habitat, put the pieces together just right and find a shed exactly where I think there should be one. And that feeling is like nothing else in the world.

Most knowledge about how to find sheds you'll probably gain on your own over a lifetime of searching as you learn about deer movements and preferred forage species in your area, but hopefully these tips will speed up the learning process.

When to Look

As mentioned in Chapter 1, whitetails may drop their antlers any time between November and May. However, the majority of bucks in North America shed their antlers roughly from late December until early March. Because shed hunting when antlers are still mobile is highly ineffective, it's obviously best to wait until some, or most, of the bucks have shed their antlers before you take up

STICKER POINT:

Shed Hunting's Golden Rules

1. Keep the sun at your back. Looking into the sun makes you squint. Plus, antlers are easier to see when they're lit by the sun. Keep the sun at your back, and shed hunt on a cloudy day after a rain when wet antlers stand out from the forest floor better.

2. Keep a positive attitude. Remain optimistic at all times, even if you're searching in an area covered with someone else's boot tracks. If you don't think you'll find anything, why bother looking?

3. Search as if you'd never been there. If you're entering an area for the first time or the 10th time this season, stay fresh. Don't assume you've found all the sheds. Come at a different angle to see things from a new perspective. Remember, you could have walked past an antler, or a buck could have shed since your last visit.

4. Stay focused. Don't let your mind wander to next weekend's fishing trip or dwell on a deadline at work. Your mind should be focused on unraveling a buck's activities, not your own.

5. Do your homework. Deer frequently winter in the same areas each year, but not always. Things can change, whether it's land development, logging or crop rotations. Keep tabs on what's going on in your shedding grounds and the surrounding areas.

6. Head south. In areas that receive at least some direct sunlight, deer almost always bed on the south side of cover to take advantage of winter rays. From a whole forest to a lone tree to a hillside, keep direction in mind and always check the southern exposure.

7. Keep quiet. It can be tempting to tell of your success, but if you want your best spots to keep producing, keep them secret.

8. Be thorough. Walk slowly, keep your eyes on the ground and check out anything that looks like a piece of an antler. If you're walking for several miles in a day, what's a few extra steps?

9. Don't give up. If you know bucks are frequenting an area, the sheds will be there. Keep at it and enlist the help of close friends if you need to. It might take weeks or even years to find a match.

10. Have fun. Search hard, find some sheds and enjoy yourself.

shed hunting in earnest for the season. You'll also want to get after antlers soon after they drop before they're buried by emerging spring vegetation or consumed by rodents.

In order to know just when most bucks have dropped their antlers, you'll have to monitor deer in your area. Not only does keeping tabs on deer throughout the winter show you when most bucks drop their antlers, it also naturally reveals *where* deer spend their time, and in effect, where the most antlers are likely to be found. You can monitor deer by backyard observations, roadside sightings, word of mouth from coworkers, scouting-camera photos, hiking trips or any number of ways. As the peak of shedding season nears I begin taking scenic evening drives through farm country where herds of deer congregate in fields. The dark forms of deer show up easily against the snow-covered landscape, and a quick scan with binoculars reveals whether deer are packing antlers or not.

Of course, it can be hard to tell from a distance, especially in low light, whether you're looking at a doe or an antlerless buck. That's why routine deer observations will help you determine when deer are shedding. If you haven't seen an antlered buck in places where you've seen them regularly throughout the winter, you may assume that perhaps the deer you *are* seeing are antlerless bucks. Spotting half-racked bucks is also a distinct possibility, and when you see such a buck, chances are good that the buck has dropped its first antler within the last few days and the other is soon to follow.

When you actually begin looking for sheds depends on several factors, and there are cases for hitting the woods early and often, as well as cases for staying out and being patient. Here are some scenarios.

First off, playing the waiting game has its merits. Weather is the most obvious reason for delaying your shed hunts. Simply put, it's hard to find antlers if they are buried under deep snow, so you may want to wait until some or all of it melts. Waiting for all the bucks to shed their antlers is another good reason for delaying your shed-hunting trips. If you're planning to hit a favorite shedding grounds far away, or simply a large cornfield that requires painfully slow row-by-row walking, your best bet is to be sure all antlers are on the ground before you try to tackle these areas. You do not want to have to walk through the same 100-acre picked cornfield twice! You may also opt to stay out of a buck haunt to avoid spooking deer out of their core areas. This is especially true if your shedding grounds are bordered by inaccessible property, or if it's the peak of the shedding season and there's a good chance a bumped buck could drop its sheds elsewhere

STICKER POINT:

My First Shed

Growing up, from time to time I'd hear about someone finding a shed antler. I found this hard to believe. It seemed few bucks survived our gun season and lived to drop antlers in the spring.

When my college roommate found three sheds, I was fascinated. That spring, my brother found two antlers while turkey hunting and that fanned the flames even more. After his hunt, we looked for sheds.

I focused my efforts in a tamarack swamp about 200 yards from my deer stand. Back and forth I hiked the heavily trodden trails. I was putting all my eggs in one basket by staring at my feet as I walked those trails, but I didn't know any better. I was walking across a road through the swamp when I spied long white objects protruding up from the grass. My heart raced, but I told myself to calm down. It really looked like an antler, but I didn't want to get my hopes up for nothing. I walked closer, and the torture of not knowing what I was looking at was practically killing me. The closer I got, the more certain I became that this was an antler. Finally, when I knew it was a shed, I raced to it, picked it up and turned it over and over in my hands. I have not yet stopped fondling that antler.

after you kick it out of the area. There are plenty of good reasons for postponing a shed hunt until the right moment. It all depends on your specific situation.

Despite these fine cases for waiting, delaying your shed hunting trips simply isn't easy, especially when your friends are finding antlers and you're dying to record that first find of the year. In truth, sometimes patience is not the best route to more sheds. This is particularly so if there is competition from other shed hunters in your best areas. In that case, it's best to hit the woods early and often so you can find fresh drops before anyone else. Keep in mind that competition isn't limited to the two-legged kind. The longer an antler lies on the ground, the better the chances it will be chewed on by some type of critter. What a shame to discover a matched set from a beautiful buck, only to find the antler tips nibbled off! If you're going to be shed hunting in places with lots of squirrels, such as in oak forests, you'd better be hitting the woods every chance you get. When shed hunting diverse areas, I'll hit oak woods and other squirrel havens first and search marshes and swamps last because squirrels usually aren't a problem in the latter areas. Lastly, remember that the longer an antler is "out there," the more weathered it will be. Eventually it will fade and crack or turn green. Also, the longer it sits the more it will sink into the forest duff or be covered by newly emerging plants.

So what's the solution – hit the woods or wait? As with most things in life, I think balance is the key. Personally I used to prefer to hit areas of competition early and often and stay the heck out of areas I knew I had to myself until I guessed all the antlers were shed and the weather was favorable. I've amended this slightly. When competition is a factor I still shed hunt as normal, but now I try to at least poke my nose into my more private areas while snow is still on the ground.

The reason why comes down to scouting. In spring, after the snow melts, trails, droppings, rubs and other deer signs are still visible, and you can learn a lot more about deer movements by heading to your best woods and swamps at least once or twice while snow still lingers on the ground. For one thing, when there's snow, you can study individual tracks and learn whether the trail is used by a big-footed buck or just a few does – a technique that becomes much more difficult in spring when all you've got to look at is a line of matted-down grass. Seeing tracks in winter positively identifies where deer travel, and being out there early reveals which areas have deep snow and which ones have little or no snow, which often has significant bearing on where deer travel. Plus, when snow is on the ground you can pinpoint beds and check them for early sheds. And lastly, although in time shed hunters develop a good feel for where deer will travel through the woods and why they choose to walk there, sometimes after seeing tracks revealed so clearly in the white stuff, I realize that my assumptions are wrong – dead wrong!

For example, in one swamp I commonly shed hunt in the spring there is a narrow island that rises about 4 feet above the surrounding terrain – just high enough to stay dry. I assumed deer stayed on top of this in winter, but when I actually ventured into the swamp one winter instead of waiting until spring, I was amazed to find that deer usually traveled on the side of the island, and frequently walked right down into the swamp bottom. Then it dawned on me that when the swamp is frozen, the walking is as good in the bottoms as it is on the island. But evidence showed that deer still preferred to bed on the island, where they apparently have a better view of their surroundings.

When should you shed hunt? It's a delicate question. One winter, after spotting a nice buck on a couple occasions during deer season, I vowed to stay out of that area until March when I was sure the buck would have dropped his headgear. Despite my best efforts that spring, I didn't locate either of his antlers. In the same season, at a place that was less than 20 acres just a few miles away, I found a freshly shed antler on February 28. I returned to this area about three times each week, looking for more sheds, and amazingly I continued to find them. All told, I picked up 10 sheds from that spot (including only one match and a whopping eight singles that I could not seem to match up). And best of all, despite my frequent trespasses into these bucks' winter lair, it didn't seem to bother them, and I found fresh sheds well into April. The catch, however, is these were all young bucks. Would I have repeatedly searched the area if I knew a large buck was wintering there? No. I'd have probably waited until April, then pounded the woods until I found the sheds or became convinced I wouldn't find them.

When should you shed hunt? Weigh your options, listen to your gut and do what feels right. Any time is a good time to be out enjoying the woods.

What to Look For

Antler hunting is in many ways like deer hunting. After all, you're trying to find areas that deer frequent, and you do that by looking for tracks and other deer sign, just like when you're deer hunting. But hunting deer has certain advantages over shed hunting. For one thing, when you're deer hunting, you can

Unlike deer hunters, shed hunters must rely almost exclusively on their eyes to find their quarry. You can literally walk past an antler in the blink of an eye.

pretty much shoot a buck whenever you can find it during the open hunting season, whether it's on a Tuesday morning or a Saturday evening. Of course, shed hunting has no established season, however, you have to find the exact location of a buck at the exact moment it dropped an antler to be successful. Therefore, shed hunting is a lot more limiting as far as distance (you have to be able to see an antler, not merely be within gun or bow range of it) and in time (you have to be in the exact spot the buck was when it dropped the antler). There are other challenges to shed hunting. For example, when hunting for deer, you can rely on more than one sense to detect them. You might see a deer burst from its bed or hear that telltale crackling of leaves that tells you a deer is approaching. But when shed hunting, you won't hear a deer snort to alert you that there's an antler lying on the ground. You have to rely almost exclusively on your eyes, unless of course you happen to step on one, but when it comes right down to it, your eyes are what unravel the mysteries of shed hunting.

One question you'll probably ask yourself is "What am I looking for?" Antlers fall in forests and cornfields. Antlers look like sticks and cornstalks. Therefore, you have to separate the proverbial grain from the chaff. Sometimes antlers will be easy to see. They'll be in the open and readily visible, like in a food plot or a harvested soybean field. But more often, they'll be much harder to see. In a forest, look for bits and pieces of an antler, just like you'd look for a leg, ear or tail before you can identify the whole deer when you're deer hunting. You're looking for that something that just doesn't look like it fits into its surroundings. Many times I've scanned the woods and my eyes have cruised right past an antler. Then, my brain kicks in and says, "Wait a minute, go back and check that out." And sure enough, when I swivel my head back to the ground I just looked at, there's an antler.

Some of the things I like to look for, rather than seeing a whole antler lying on the ground, are a curving main beam, a base pointed toward you, or more likely, a tine projecting a few inches above the forest duff. I often photograph sheds that I find before I pick them up so I can study how they lay and train myself to better pick out sheds from their surroundings. Antlers can land tines up or tines

At a glance, antlers look very much like cornstalks and branches. Walking slowly will help you identify sheds.

Sometimes antlers land tines up, and sometimes they land tines down. It's a function of ground composition, antler configuration and chance. Tines-up sheds are easier to see.

down. Sometimes I actually hold them up to simulate how they would be on a buck's head, then drop them to see how they fall. I suppose the way antlers land when they fall off a buck's head depends on the way their weight is dispersed, the softness or hardness of the ground and any bouncing action the ground causes, and also the characteristics of antler tines that could cause the antlers to flip upon impact. Sometimes you'll find very symmetrical matched sets lying side by side, and one antler is tines up, while the other is orientated tines down. I'm probably over-thinking this whole thing, but I do know this much: according to my shed-hunting journal, 68 percent of the antlers I find are tines up. Does this mean they have a tendency to land this way? Maybe, but not necessarily. My assumption is this: antlers probably land tines up about half of the time, but they're easier to see because of the tines sticking up, and that's why I find more antlers with their tines pointing up.

The bottom line is, if I see anything that looks like an antler, I check it out, even if I think it's probably just a stick. My philosophy is this: if I'm spending hours on end walking through the woods, I'm not going to miss out on finding a shed

Tossing a shed and trying to find it can keep you sharp, especially on those days when you just can't seem to find anything. Just don't chuck the antler too far!

because I was too lazy to take a few extra steps and positively identify something that looks like an antler. In the same vein, anytime I step on something that feels like a stick, I stop and check to see if that stick is really an antler, especially if it doesn't break underfoot as I step on it. Using these techniques and sticking to them has greatly increased the number of antlers I find each year.

Many times I've found an antler that I know I've passed within feet of before without seeing it, and I shudder at the thought of how many sheds I've walked right past that are now rotting on the forest floor. But over time, as you get used to picking out antlers, you will become more adept at spotting them. One way to shorten your learning curve is to practice seeing them. On days when you don't have time to shed hunt, or on those slow shedding days when you're in need of some excitement, practicing can be just the ticket. Toss an antler out into grass, brush or woods without watching where it lands, then try to find it. Doing so will help keep you sharp. Antlers are durable, and you shouldn't have to worry about breaking it, as long as it's a fresh shed. Just be careful you don't throw it too far. There's more than one story of the shed hunter who couldn't find a tossed antler, so don't overdo it! Also be sure not to chuck it too high. If it lands in a tree, and you think it's on the ground, you may never find it!

As simple as this exercise sounds, it can be challenging. When my friend Ryan found his first antler, he left it where it lay, then challenged our friend Nick to find it. After more than 15 minutes of searching, Nick didn't believe that Ryan had actually found an antler, and finally told him to prove it. Ryan retrieved the shed, which was only 15 yards away, and Nick has been hooked on shed hunting ever since.

In order to thoroughly search an area, walk s-l-o-w-l-y. Some people disagree with this philosophy. They believe that you have to cover ground to find antlers, which is true. However, I believe it's critical to give each area a good look, especially if you want to find the tiny antlers I'm so good at finding! Besides, it makes more sense to cover a smaller amount of area thoroughly than to cover a larger area but miss most of the antlers.

My eyes cannot effectively scan my surroundings fast enough at a normal gait, so I slow down and really concentrate on what is on the ground before me. I typically scan no more than about 10 yards in front of me, however, this varies depending on terrain. If it's more open, you can obviously look farther in front of you, and vice versa. It doesn't pay to look too far ahead, because you'll cover that ground when you walk forward.

STICKER POINT:

Slow Down!

What pace should you be walking at? Just because you're not finding antlers doesn't necessarily mean you're walking too fast to see them. There simply may not be any to see. However, keep these thoughts in mind. In any given deer population, there will be more young bucks with small racks than older bucks with larger racks. Granted, in many areas, especially those areas that receive heavy hunting pressure, large-racked bucks may be hard to come by. In the event that there are a fair number of older bucks in your area and you're finding large sheds but few or no small sheds, you're probably walking too fast. Granted, if you're finding larger sheds, you may not care about finding the small ones. Unfortunately, not everyone has this problem, simply because many people shed hunt in areas with few older bucks. Here's another consideration: in the brushy and wooded areas where I shed hunt most often, I find mostly antlers from yearling bucks, whether they're spikes, small 4-points or somewhere in between. On average, I spot these antlers at a distance of only 10 feet; sometimes farther, sometimes closer. It stands to reason that to find these small sheds you must be walking slowly and thoroughly scanning an area. The bottom line is if you're in an area that looks promising and you're not finding sheds, slow down!

Occasionally I stop if I think the area needs to be covered more thoroughly, or my eyes are getting tired. I wear contact lenses, and my eyes get tired after long periods of maintaining my "blank stare" in which I see everything at once and nothing in particular. This wasn't the case when I wore glasses. Sometimes it pays to just take a moment, look up, and blink a few times before resuming, especially if you have to drive home.

It's important to pay attention to deer sign as you walk. Look for old rubs that indicate a buck uses the area. Watch for beds located just off the trail. But keep in mind, you're always looking for sheds, too. When you see noteworthy deer sign, stop so you can properly examine it without compromising your search for antlers.

Occasionally it pays to look up for antlers. Yes, I'm well aware that deer don't fly, but before you say I've spent too much time aimlessly wandering the woods, hear me out. Sometimes when a buck walks through a particularly brushy area, an antler will become snagged in brush and detach from its head. But rather than falling to the ground, it remains caught in the brush, and suspended in the air. When you find your first "hanger," you've found a real trophy! Squirrels also sometimes move antlers off the ground. Squirrels, which are just one of the many animals that chew on antlers for their mineral content, will drag antlers to their den trees so the antler is more readily accessible for gnawing. Also, if the antler is small enough, rodents will sometimes actually drag it up the tree! Ground-dwelling critters also move antlers around. Pocket gophers and foxes sometimes carry sheds to their burrows, so any time you find such a den, check the immediate area – and even the burrow itself – for antlers. Rodents will actually eat antlers, but foxes only gnaw on them like a dog would, so antlers around fox dens are likely to be in relatively decent shape, if a bit smelly, because foxes may decide to urinate on their chew toys.

You won't always find antlers on the ground. Sometimes bucks shed when their antlers snag on brush.

When you find an especially good-looking area to shed hunt, breaking down the area into a grid can help you cover the ground more thoroughly. A grid search isn't something you probably want to do all the time because it's extremely time-consuming and limits the amount of ground you can cover. However, if you find a promising spot, or if you've located an antler and want to find the match, you can systematically cover the area, ensuring that you haven't missed anything.

To do a grid search, walk in a straight line to a predetermined point. Then, slide over a few feet and walk back to your starting point. The key is to make each pass close together, as if you were walking up and down cornrows. In theory, you should be able to cover every square inch of real estate in the area you are searching. In open cover you might be moving 25 feet with each pass; in thick stuff, you might be moving only 5.

When grid searching, be attentive and thorough. One of the best shed hunters I know once told me, "If you're not walking into trees every once in a while, you're not doing it right!"

This brings up another good point. Even if you're not walking into big pines or oaks, you are certainly going to get pricked, prodded and poked by branches and thorns. In fact, I once stepped on a stick, which catapulted mud into my eye like something out of a Three Stooges act. This left me rubbing my eye for a good half-hour, and I actually had to take my contact lens out in the field and clean the mud out of it. But the good news is this happened when I was walking toward one of those "suspicious-looking sticks," that turned out to be an antler. The point is, it might not be a bad idea to wear sunglasses or even safety glasses while you shed hunt. I'm not going to be your mother and nag you for not wearing some type of eye protection in the woods, but it's a lot harder to find sheds when you've got a patch over one eye.

One more tip: pay attention to the weather. If there's a foot of fresh snow on the ground, it's obviously going to be mighty tough to find antlers, but consider other weather conditions, such as rain and clouds. Many folks say that hands-down, their favorite conditions for shed hunting are overcast skies just after a rain. Rain offers a couple of advantages to the shed hunter. First, it packs down leaves and grass, making antlers stand out from the surrounding vegetation. Second, a wet antler has a certain shine to it that fallen branches don't have. Clouds are helpful too. It may seem sunny days would be best for antler hunting, as the sun would create that same shiny look on an antler, and in open areas, that may be true. However, in wooded areas, the sun also casts uncountable shadows that tend to camouflages antlers. Plus, the glare of the sun causes you to squint, which makes it harder to effectively search for antlers.

Where to Look

The question of where to look for antlers is a multi-layered one. You have to pick an area that bucks frequent during late winter and early spring and eliminate unproductive areas. You also have to have a physical chunk of land on which to look for antlers, and in this day of private-land ownership, access may pose a problem.

If you're a deer hunter, you'll obviously want to search for sheds on your hunting grounds. Any antlers you find will tell you where a buck spends his time during the winter, which may or may not help you during hunting season, depending on whether or not he makes a seasonal migration to a wintering area. What a shed antler *will* tell you, at the very least, is that a given buck has survived the winter. Chances are good that he will be around during the fall when hunting season rolls around, and he'll probably be wearing a larger set of headgear.

However, you don't have to be a deer hunter to enjoy walking through the woods and searching for antlers. Even if you are a deer hunter, that doesn't restrict you to searching only your hunting grounds. I'm constantly searching for new places to shed hunt, which is frequently easier than actually finding antlers, just because I enjoy walking in the woods during the spring and the excitement of finding an antler.

When looking for places to shed hunt, search for a place that satisfies two basic criteria: a high deer population and low hunting pressure. This combination ensures there will be a decent amount of sheds to find. For this reason, seek out areas that can't be hunted, such as heavily wooded urban parks, paper company land that is not open to hunting, state-owned lands that are open to fishing but not hunting and even golf courses. Other places such as state parks, wildlife sanctuaries or some natural areas might be good places to try as well, but they might not allow removal of natural objects, including sheds. However, that doesn't stop some die-hard shed hunters. Some people will actually search areas that are closed to collecting natural objects, and when they find a shed, they simply take a picture and leave it where they found it. This "catch and release" shed hunting is certainly an alternative to not shed hunting at all, but most people want to feel the weight of an antler in hand, and admire it on a shelf at home. But to each his own.

Deer hunting is usually better on private lands than on public lands because there are generally more deer and fewer hunters to reduce the deer population. However, in many areas, it seems the days of free-by-permission deer hunting are over, as more people become sick of dealing with crowded public areas and buy their own hunting land, and economic pressure forces farmers to lease out their lands to hunters to help make ends meet. But acquiring permission to shed hunt isn't nearly as difficult. In fact, many farmers welcome shed hunters for one very simple reason: antlers can wreak havoc on farm equipment. The following scenario plays out countless times each spring: a farmer drives his tractor through a field, runs over an antler, and it lodges in his tire, leading to expensive repairs. Or, an antler may become lodged in another piece of farm machinery, such as

Not everyone likes finding antlers. Sheds that lodge in tractor tires and other farm implements can cause costly repairs. Find a farmer who has suffered antler damage and you may have free reign of his property each spring.

Although free-by-permission deer hunting is a thing of the past in many areas, farmers often don't mind if people shed hunt their property.

a corn picker. If you find a farmer who has experienced such problems, you're likely to have free reign of his property each spring.

If you're having trouble gaining access to places where deer are plentiful, you can always try public hunting areas. The downside is heavy hunting pressure tends to thin out the deer herd, but hunters never shoot all the deer. One of my most satisfying finds was the first antler I ever found on land owned by our state department of natural resources, just a mile out of town. Although the antler was small, I knew that the buck had survived three and a half months of heavy hunting pressure on public land. What's more, I found the antler lying between two improvised ground blinds sitting only 30 yards apart! These days, nearly all my sheds come from public land. Not only have they become some of my most frequent shedding grounds, but given the sheer number of antlers I've found on them, public hunting grounds have instilled in me a belief that they aren't the wildlife deserts they are so often made out to be, and I find myself deer hunting in them more each year.

Private-Land Quality on Public Ground

If the idea of shed hunting public land leaves you cold, and you'd rather spend time searching private agricultural lands where deer numbers are higher, maybe all you need to do is a little homework. In some cases, state natural resources agencies

One of the author's most rewarding finds was the first shed he found while shed hunting on heavily hunted public land.

You don't have to own land to enjoy good shed hunting. Public lands that don't allow deer hunting can be great places to look.

plant agricultural crops specifically left unharvested for wildlife on publicly owned lands. Ask your local wildlife biologist if there are planted crops on any public lands in your area.

Another option is to shed hunt on public lands that abut private agricultural properties. In this scenario, deer will often bed in the protective cover on public land and venture into private farm fields to feed at night. Seek out thick bedding areas or transitional staging areas on public ground for the best shed-hunting opportunities. In some cases, you'll discover that public land can be every bit as good as private land for shed hunting.

Keep Your Eyes Peeled

Always be on the lookout for new shedding grounds. I once searched a parcel of land owned by the city public works department that was overrun with deer, and some people even search in cemeteries! Think about where you commonly see deer as you're driving. Talk to people about where they see deer, even if they're not the deer-hunting type, and don't be afraid to ask for permission to search for antlers. The worst someone can say is no, and who knows, you may find an antler gold mine and make a new friend in the process. A situation involving one of my co-workers illustrates this point nicely. She frequently sees bucks in the back yard of her 2-acre wooded lot. Deer hang out in her yard because the neighboring area is a heavily hunted parcel of public land. Also, deer make frequent use of her garden and bird feeders. She is not a deer hunter, but she knows the habits of the bucks on her lot because she enjoys watching wildlife, and as a result, her small property has yielded multiple sheds.

Once you've got a place to explore for sheds, key in on specific areas where deer are likely to spend most of their time or will somehow have a better chance of shedding. Again, because deer spend a lot of time eating and resting in winter, check feeding and bedding areas, especially the southern exposure of a hillside or the south side of any forest edge or lone tree. Also consider places where a buck is likely to lose an antler from a jar to the body or because of contact with brush or low-hanging limbs. Check fence crossings, trails on steep embankments, creek crossings, fallen logs on trails and anyplace else where a buck might jump over an obstacle and knock off an antler. Also pay attention to trails going through thick brush or with low-hanging branches. To borrow a fishing term, these are the "spots on the spot" once you've got a parcel of land to search for sheds.

Searching Crop Fields

There's no doubt that agricultural fields are prime places to seek sheds. Crops high in carbohydrates, such as corn and soybeans, are excellent high-energy foods – far better than most natural browse – and thus are important winter food sources.

Deer eat a variety of crops in winter. Alfalfa fields are particularly good, and if the snow becomes too deep, deer will even pick away at hay bales.

Using binoculars from a high vantage point can save you a lot of walking.

In winter, deer are forced to strike a balance between food and shelter to survive. Where deer subsist entirely on natural browse, they seek thick protective cover to reduce the amount of energy needed to stay warm. However, in agricultural areas, deer may forego the best shelter in order to be closer to high-energy food sources. In fact, deer will even bed in open fields in below-zero weather if the food source is a good one. Adult bucks in particular will bed farther from thermal cover. Because they are larger than does, adult bucks lose heat more slowly, due to their lower ratio of body weight to surface area.

Deer will feed on any number of crops in winter, but corn, alfalfa, winter wheat and rye grass, just to name a few, are all highly preferred foods.

Even if several fields of the same crop exist in an area, there are a few things that help make one field stand out from the rest. First off, if a field is left unharvested, whether intentionally for wildlife or accidentally, there will obviously be more food for deer in that particular field. I once watched a soybean field that flooded in late fall. There was standing water in the lowest area of the field, and the farmer couldn't get the beans off. That winter, the low spot in the field was a deer magnet.

Other factors can make fields, or even portions of fields, more attractive. For instance, in late winter I was searching among some pine trees bordering a narrow picked cornfield. There was still more than a foot of snow on the field, but there was only an inch or two under the pines. I planned to search the field after the snow melted, so I tried to analyze the best places to search. On the north side, I could see corn stubble poking up through the snow, but the south side of the field was a solid blanket of white. The reason for this was twofold. First, although there were tall pines on both edges of the field, on the south side, the trees block the field from the sun. However, on the north side, there's nothing to shade the field. This acts on the same principle as a south-facing hillside: the

Fields left standing over the winter are especially attractive to deer. Also note the sheltering pines in the background.

STICKER POINT:

Something Different

I often liken shed antler location to trying to score a goal in hockey. Professional hockey goalies are amazingly good at stopping shots on goal – even those 90 mph slapshots that would send most ordinary folks diving for safety. How do you put a puck past someone who stops more than 90 percent of the shots he faces? You need to do something out of the ordinary. Many goals are scored when a player shoots while the goalie's vision is obscured by another player, when a player redirects a shot with his stick in mid-air, on the power play when one team has a man advantage or on a fast breakaway. It's that something different that beats the goalie.

When shed hunting, you should also look for that "something different." Because whitetails are creatures of the edge, that something different is often a place where two or more habitat types come together. Look for sheds in the brushy transition between field and forest, at the confluence of several ridge trails or along a small hardwood island in the middle of a low conifer swamp. These are the kinds of places that deer are likely to relate to.

Likewise, when you've searched up and down a likely spot where you're sure there are antlers but you've come up empty, try to come at it from a different angle, or search the areas that look least appealing. If there's competition in the area, other shed seekers may have hit the most likely areas and passed up some of the less-obvious places. Maybe try hitting these less-appealing areas. It may be the edge you need to succeed.

You can find sheds just about anywhere, just as you can sneak a shot past a goalie at any minute of the game at even strength. But the task is always easier when you find that "something different."

field is exposed to the sun's rays on the north side, and the snow melts here first. Second, the predominant wind direction is from the north, therefore, the wind would carry snow to the south side of the field. The north side is sheltered from the snow-carrying wind by the pines. I walked across the field in my hiking boots while my snowshoes sat back in my truck, and believe me, there was a definite difference in snow depth from north to south.

Setting out to search a large crop field can be daunting. There is a lot of ground to cover, and antlers could be anywhere. Before you head out, there are a few tricks you can employ to help you find antlers faster. First, if possible, keep an eye on the field. Watch where deer enter the field, and what areas of the field they feed in most often. Even if this is not possible, you'll probably be able to see tracks, either in snow or mud. Find the largest concentration of tracks and hit that spot first.

Before you even muddy your hiking boots, glass the field with binoculars. This is especially productive if the antlers in the field are large, the stubble is low or the field is just starting to green up. Getting a higher vantage point, whether you're standing on a hill or your pickup, helps. Also, it might be helpful to drive a pickup or an ATV through the field. It sure cuts down on the time spent searching, but it's not always feasible, due to muddy fields or tall crops. Sometimes you just have to resort to good old-fashioned boot leather. If so, enlist the help of a friend or two, or a shed dog (to be discussed later).

After you've tried all the shed hunting tricks you can think of, it all comes down to simple walking. Take just a few rows at a time, and walk a small section at a time, marking where you've been. It's easier and faster to look in one direction than to sweep back and forth. Be thorough, go slowly and wait until you're sure most deer have shed before undertaking such a large endeavor

Picking Apart a Woodlot

Shed hunting, in some ways, is a lot like fishing. Whether you're shedding or angling, sometimes you get skunked. Despite that hard truth, a more important connection between fishing and shedding is in the way you go about these activities. When you're fishing, you don't simply begin casting to just any old spot on the lake. You might look at a lake map, or cast to a visible rock, log, or weedbed. Shed hunting is the same way. Rather than walking back and forth through the woods, be like a fisherman and look for structure; in this case, thick brush, lone pines and other places that stick out from their surroundings.

Pick the woods apart and try to determine where bucks would spend most of their time. It often takes a lot of time to find an antler. Therefore, you should maximize your time by searching in the high-percentage areas, and going to other areas only if you have extra time or have reason to believe there are antlers there. Using this method, you will, of course, miss antlers, but you're going to miss some with any method. It's all about maximizing your opportunities.

To help you along, here's a rough map (see Page 80) of a place where I've had good success finding antlers (and no, I'm not saying where it is!) As I describe this area, I'll also show you my thought process of how and why I search the area the way I do.

This parcel is a real area that includes many deer-attracting features. Obviously not all areas are going to have the same mix of terrain features this one has, but use it as a guide to help you in your quest for better shedding grounds and as a way of learning how to dissect the landscape for likely shedding areas.

This 40-acre plot consists mostly of an open hardwood swamp on the southern two-thirds of the area. A small creek runs east and west about one-third of the way from the northern boundary. North of the creek is a small, grassy field, then a thick, narrow strip of tag alders on the northwest edge and a row of mature planted white pines on the northeast edge.

Just as important as the physical description of this area, however, is the description of the surrounding land. Although shed hunters are limited by access to private lands, deer certainly aren't, and we're trying to get a feel for how deer move through the area. You should always consider the big picture as you pick apart a shedding area. In this particular case, the surrounding lands play a key role. To the east and west of this 40-acre shedding grounds lies essentially more of the same type of hardwood swamp. The real key that makes this place attractive to bucks, however, lies in the large private cornfields to the north and south of the property. Deer can feed in the fields at night, and hide out in the woods by day.

The first thing I like to do is eliminate all the variables I can. On this parcel I ignore most of the southern two-thirds of the area, with the exception of the southern edge. Will I miss sheds? Maybe, but I'm eliminating a large portion of the parcel in an area where deer spend little time because they are just passing through – not bedding or feeding. By doing this you save a lot of time so you can more thoroughly cover the remaining areas.

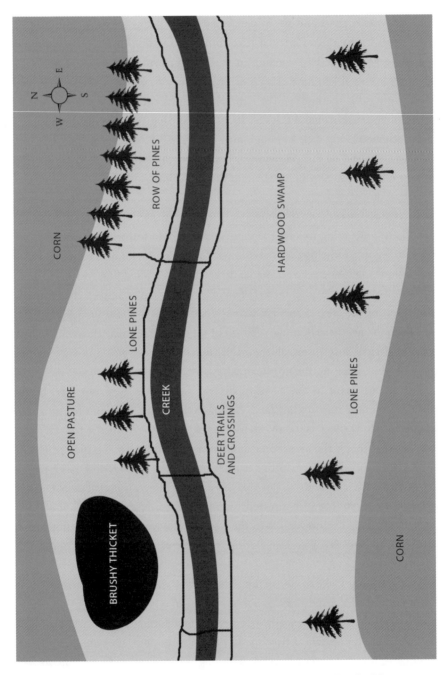

This 40-acre parcel of public land is surprisingly productive for shed hunting.

Here is how I search this parcel:

1. *I like to hit the southern edge of the woods, right along the cornfield. Here, deer have quick access to a prime food source, and they can soak up direct sunlight. In particular, I search under the few scattered tall pines here, which stand out from the surrounding hardwoods.*

2. *The row of pines on the north edge of the property is also a good spot for the same reason. Again, deer are close to the corn and the open field on the south edge of the row of pines allows deer to bed in the sunlight.*

3. *The tag alder/willow thicket on this property is a buck magnet. It measures only about 100 yards long by 20 yards wide, but it contains dozens of rubs. It's obvious that bucks love this area. Like the pine row, deer can bed along the southern edge for sun exposure, but this thicket provides a lot more cover, which is not only good for deer, but for shed hunters as well because there's a better chance of a buck snagging an antler and dropping it here. Also, from the southern edge of the thicket, I can scan the small open field for antlers that fall as deer walk toward the alders or feed on grass.*

4. *I absolutely love lone pines. Not only do they look beautiful, but they are attractive to bucks. I think this odd item on the landscape attracts deer the same way fish are attracted to a rock or log on an otherwise featureless bottom. I go out of my way to always check them out.*

5. *There are several deer trails running both parallel and perpendicular to the creek. I check every creek crossing for antlers because the jumping sometimes jars antlers loose. I also walk up and down the parallel trails because they are used quite heavily.*

6. *Lastly, I walk trails linking the south edge of the property with all the activity on the north edge.*

This 40-acre slice of shed heaven has rewarded me with a good number of sheds. Find a prime-looking parcel, pick it apart and you're well on your way to success. Oh, and if the task of finding a prime-looking parcel sounds somewhat oversimplified, I should mention this particular parcel is open to public hunting! All it takes is a little map work and legwork to find an area like this.

Searching in Snow Country

When you've got a place to shed hunt, your first task is to locate bucks. Snow cover is very helpful if you've got it, but you can certainly find bucks without it. Snow tells you a lot quickly, so if possible, try to hit the woods before the snow melts, but after it has receded enough to reveal antlers. Snow not only shows you where deer are concentrated; it also shows you where they're not. This will help you narrow your search. Keep in mind that just because an area is littered with tracks doesn't mean there will be antlers there. You might be right in the middle of a doe group's core area. Bucks frequently (but not always) separate themselves from does in winter, sometimes reforming old bachelor groups. How do you know if you're in buck territory? Watch for buck sign. Look for fresh rubs on trees. You may also see a buck's antler imprints in the snow when he feeds. Notice urine. A doe burns a hole in snow as she urinates. A buck is more likely to spray urine, and he'll often dribble as he walks. Many people say they can tell a buck's track because he leaves drag marks in the snow. A word of caution, however. All deer will leave drag marks in deep snow. This trick is more reliable when there's only an inch or two of the white stuff on the ground, and even then it's not infallible. Experienced deer trackers may also be able to tell a buck's track by it's wider spacing, both laterally and between tracks. However, this is applicable only to mature bucks. There are certainly trackers out there who can fairly reliably tell a buck's track from a doe's, but I'm not one of them. Urine patterns, rubs and antler imprints in the snow are much more reliable gender indicators.

Big-Woods Shed Hunting

Searching large tracts of woods for antlers can be daunting. "How am I going to find something as small as an antler in such a large area?" you may ask yourself.

I must admit, I've asked myself this question many times. One time I encountered a large swamp, and the sheer thought of trying to search it for antlers seemed hopeless. Indeed, the first time I searched it I found nothing. However, the forest's sheer size told me there had to be deer there. On the return trip, I promised myself to search it smartly, by checking the best areas, rather than ambling blindly through the woods, hoping to haphazardly stumble on an antler. I began searching the edges, where deer were likely to stage before leaving the woods to feed in neighboring agricultural fields under the cover of darkness.

Snow can tell you a lot about deer behavior, deer movements and even the sex of deer in the area.

I then followed a tiny stream – a deer magnet – deep into the gullet of the dark, eerie swamp. Both these places – the edges and the stream banks – produced sheds on that second trip. I then began to pick the area apart more, taking well-established trails from the staging areas, following them across the stream and into a clearing in the forest where deer could lie on the high ground and soak up the winter sun. Like magic I had unlocked several secrets of that forest, and ended up finding quite a few antlers. In fact, that forest – a place I expected to find no antlers at first – produced fully half of the antlers I found that entire season.

A large, unbroken forest is likely home to a lot of deer, due to its size – not necessarily its deer density – and there should be antlers to find in it. But you wouldn't hunt deer by painstakingly trying to roust them from every featureless nook and cranny, so why try to shed hunt it that way? Pick terrain features that attract deer. Pay attention to food sources. Look for natural funnels such as saddles connecting two ridges that concentrate deer movements. This is how you pick apart a large forest.

Keep the essentials in mind. Deer need food. Are there any clear-cuts in the area that would provide browse within easy reach for deer? Also, look for mast-bearing trees or preferred browse species. If you find concentrations of these food items, you'll also find concentrations of deer. Depending on your local weather, water can be important too. In warmer regions, creeks, lakes or even puddles can draw deer. Even in colder regions, some streams remain ice-free throughout the winter and can attract deer. Regardless of the presence of open water, plant communities found along streams and beaver ponds often provide browse and thick cover for deer.

Watch terrain features that direct deer movement. Natural funnels, bands of thick cover in sparsely forested areas and other terrain features alter deer movement. Exposed sunny spots or evergreens in a hardwood swamp attract bedding deer. Keep in mind that just because there are no agricultural fields, houses or roads breaking up a large tract of forest, deer relate to them just like they relate to any other area, so watch for classic shed-hunting spots, such as south-facing slopes. Look for concentrations of deer tracks, rubs and other sign, and avoid areas devoid of tracks and deer sign. Too often, people spend too much time in featureless terrain, assuming that just because they are in the woods, there will be sheds there. The smart shed hunter picks apart the cover, searching the best-looking places effectively and efficiently, and searches the remainder of the area only if time allows or when searching for a match.

Blood Trailing for Sheds

Sometimes, instead of finding an antler, you may discover tiny drops of blood in the snow. When I find a small blood trail, which usually consists of tiny, well-spaced specks of blood, my heart starts racing. Chances are the blood is from a buck's pedicel, which is bleeding because the buck recently shed an antler, exposing an open wound on the buck's head. Obviously, you'll want to backtrack the buck. Despite the large wounds buck incur on their heads after shedding, little blood actually falls to the ground. The pedicels begin scabbing over almost immediately and heal very quickly, otherwise there would be significant die-off among bucks as a result of infection during the shedding season.

It certainly pays to follow a blood trail, both to backtrack it for the cast antler, and follow it forward for the possibility of finding the second antler. However, surprisingly, finding the shed antler that caused the bleeding isn't always a sure thing. I've followed such trails before and come up empty. I'm not sure why this is. Perhaps the bleeding lasts a day or two, and the buck puts on significant mileage between casting and depositing the blood trail. Perhaps the trail is left because the buck reopens the wound somehow. Nevertheless, following a blood trail is always worthwhile.

5
You Found One!

Y ou've been slogging through thick conifer swamps and across picked cornfields for days. You're tired, sore and losing faith in this ridiculous quest for antlers, which you've decided probably don't even exist. Suddenly, you spot a pointy white object jutting up through tall yellow grass under a bushy white pine. "It could be a stick," you think to yourself, not wanting to get your hopes up, only to have them dashed for the umpteenth time. But this time, something tells you things are different. "Why would there be a white stick under a pine tree?" you think as you quicken your pace. Then, when you're 10 feet away, you see other pointed objects, arranged along a curving main beam. An antler! Let the celebration begin!

No matter how many sheds you find, this scenario never gets old. Big or small, antlers are just too uncommon to be taken lightly, whether you find one each year or 100. Savor the moment, but remember, unless you were lucky enough to find both sides of a rack side by side, there's a matching antler out there somewhere just waiting to be found. Take note of what you've got in hand, then look for that match!

◀ *Finding a shed antler is exciting!*

What Have You Found?

When you've finally got an antler in hand, you're probably going to have some questions. If you're a deer hunter whose tag went unfilled last fall, your first question is likely to be "Where was this buck last fall?" Joking aside, there's a lot of information to be gleaned from a shed. The first thing is to try to determine how long it's been sitting on the ground. The first thing to check for is blood on the base of the antler. The wetter the blood, the fresher the find, but if you find any blood at all, chances are the antler was shed within a few days or maybe up to a week. At any rate, that antler is fresh!

Barring blood, the biggest determinant of age is the presence of a skin ring. When an antler drops off a buck's head, a narrow ring of skin remains on the base of the antler, toward the outer edge of the base, just inside the burr. It's the only flesh you'll find on the antler, and sometimes there will be a small amount of hair with it. If left in the elements, this ring quickly decays, and on a year-old shed, you'll never even know it was there.

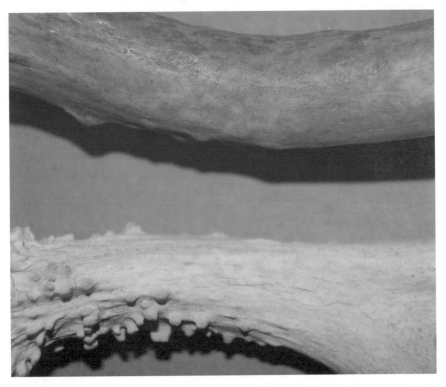

A freshly shed antler has a glossy sheen (top) while an older antler appears faded.

The skin ring, which is found around the base of freshly cast antlers, is the only flesh you'll find on a shed. A skin ring remains on an antler longer than blood, but it rots away after a few weeks.

The antler's shine is another indication of freshness or lack thereof. If it's a fresh antler, dropped within the last few months, it will have a glossy sheen to it, just like that found on the antlers of live or freshly killed bucks. Color isn't a reliable indicator because antler color varies so much. Western Canadian deer are famous for their deep chocolate-brown racks, but elsewhere bucks may carry antlers that are almost pure white. Antlers will fade after they fall to the ground, but in open areas, they will actually fade while they're still on the buck, so color won't tell you much. The only reliable clue color can give you is this: if the antler is white on the side facing up when you found it, but darker or stained below, it's been on the ground a while. If it's white on both sides, it probably bleached while still on the deer's head. Due to color inconsistencies, the glossy sheen is the thing to look for.

Although they may look cute, squirrels are the No. 1 enemy of shed hunters. Squirrels and other rodents chew on antlers for their mineral content.

Soon after antlers drop, a variety of critters will nibble away on them, seeking the minerals – mainly calcium and phosphorus – antlers contain. Mice, squirrels and porcupines are the most notorious culprits, but it's been reported that even deer will chomp on antlers. The longer an antler sits on the ground, the greater the chance something will chew on it, and it's amazing what a small set of rodent teeth can do to tough, bony appendages that have scarred trees and clashed against other bucks. Within days, squirrels and other creatures may find antlers and begin gnawing through them, usually starting at the tips of the tines. If the antler falls in an oak forest, where squirrels are abundant, the antler may be consumed in a matter of weeks. In other areas where rodents are absent or uncommon, an antler can remain on the ground for years.

But they don't last forever. Even if they're not consumed, the affects of weather will take their toll on antlers. Within months, the natural sheen fades away, replaced by a dry surface. Sunlight soon bleaches the antler. Often an antler that's been sitting for a while will be bleached on the side that was pointed up, while the bottom side exhibits a somewhat normal color, although the underside may be stained from leaves or algal growth. If the antler falls in a moist area, it

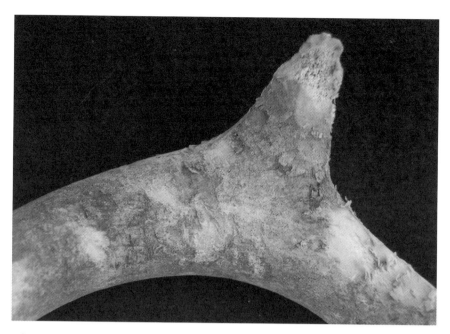

This antler has not only been chewed on, but algal growth has turned it green.

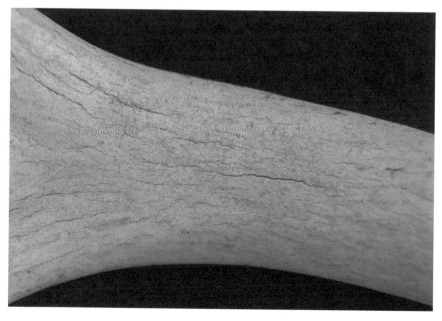

Sun exposure has bleached this antler and caused it to crack lengthwise.

will gradually turn green and porous. In arid regions, the antler turns white, then becomes dry and brittle, and it will begin to crack lengthwise. It may take years – maybe even more than a decade – but in time, the antler will return to the soil it sits on. For these reasons, it may be wise to search oak forests and other places where rodents are numerous earlier in the season, and places like swamps, which often preserve antlers for years, later on.

The Matched Set

The best thing about finding antlers is they come in pairs, so when you find one, you can be confident that not only are you in a buck's wintering area, but there is at least one more antler waiting to be found.

Finding matched sets is one of the biggest thrills of shed hunting. Only finding several successive years of matched sets from the same buck or shooting a buck whose sheds you've found could top finding a matched set.

The author's shed hunting partner Nick Morehouse found this beautiful matched set in February. Squirrels had already done considerable damage to the buck's right antler, and Nick reported squirrel trails in the snow leading from the right antler directly to several different trees.

Matching up a set of sheds can be ridiculously easy or excruciatingly difficult. Sometimes both antlers fall off together. Sometimes they fall off a few feet apart. Quite often, they drop on different days, and therefore, end up being several hundred yards or even miles apart.

If the matching antler isn't within just a few feet of the first antler, try to determine the buck's travel pattern as he moved through the area. Go up and down the trail 100 yards in both directions. Although that's not a lot of real estate, in thick cover, it can be a real chore. Go slowly and look carefully. If you miss that little bit of tine sticking up from an obstruction, you could be looking at hours of fruitless searching in the wrong spot. If you don't find the match, go back to the site of the find and sweep the area with concentric circles, studying the ground carefully. You might enlist the help of a friend to cover the ground more effectively. If your circle stretches 100 yards from the antler and you're confident you've thoroughly covered the ground without finding the match, you probably won't find it within the vicinity. The match may still be atop the buck's head, or it might be far from the first one. Don't get disheartened. Even the best antler seekers find matched sets less than 50 percent of the time. Finding antlers wouldn't be fun if it were easy. All you can do is try to analyze what the deer was doing when it shed, where it was going, where it was coming from and other pertinent information. Search hard and don't give up. Many are the stories of sets of antlers that were matched up weeks or even years after the first shed was found! Keep searching until you find the match, you learn that someone else has found it or you finally get tired of the hunt and give up.

Besides the difficulty of simply finding two antlers, determining whether you have a matched set can be tough. Quite often, a left and a right side will be essentially mirror images of each other. However, this isn't always the case. Most deer hunters realize that 7-point bucks and 9-point bucks are pretty common. In the case of a 9 pointer, this usually means that you're looking at a buck with 4 points on one side and 5 on the other, although other configurations are certainly possible. Often, the "extra" point on one side will be relatively short. In the case of a 9-pointer, for example, the G-4 on the 5-point side is often somewhat shorter in proportion to the rest of the tines. If this is the case, ignore this oddball point and compare the other four points on the 5-point side to the opposite 4-point antler. If they match up well in terms of tine length and tine configuration, you've likely got a match. Also, compare other traits, such as color, the amount of mass, size and shape of the antler bases, the amount of beading toward the

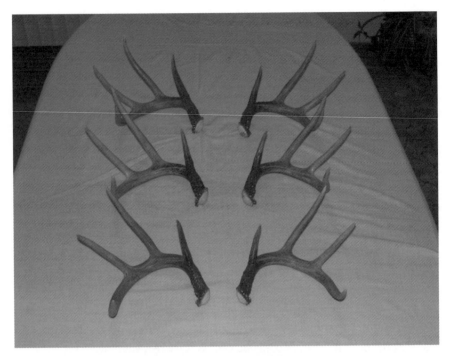

In shed hunting, the only things better than finding a matched set are finding several years of matched sets from the same buck, or even better, finding multiple sets from the same buck and eventually bagging the deer.

base of the antler and any other distinguishing characteristics that the antlers have in common. It also helps to know the genetics in your local deer herd. For example, in one of my shedding areas, yearling bucks frequently grow racks with 3 points on the left side, two on the right, and no brow tines. Before I realized this, I was having a hard time finding "matches." However, seeing live bucks, and finding a dead buck in the woods helped me study this configuration, and I've learned that several bucks in this area grow these 5-point racks as yearlings, likely as a result of genetics. Seeing live bucks will certainly help you determine antler patterns, but an even better resource is a photograph because it lets you study racks anytime you want. Scouting cameras do an excellent job of recording individual deer in the area, and having an actual photograph of a buck's rack and antler configuration make it much easier to determine whether you have a matched set. In fact, some racks are so asymmetrical that it would be impossible to know the two antlers were a match if you didn't see the buck or a photo of it.

STICKER POINT:

The Ultimate Challenge

Serious deer hunters who do a lot of scouting and have a good understanding of when and how deer move on their hunting property sometimes take their hunting to a higher level by targeting a particular buck with their gun or bow. The same is true of shed hunters.

Perhaps shed hunters target specific bucks more frequently, but that may be because shed hunters have no bag limits, and any buck with antlers to drop come spring is fair game in the eyes of a shed hunter. However, quite often, people try to find sheds off of one particular buck. It's often a monster buck that the shed hunter has encountered through scouting-camera photos, in-the-field sighting or close encounters during hunting season. Looking for sheds from such a buck may take precedence over all else and can border on an obsession. In fact, many people spend days, weeks or months trying to find antlers from a specific buck. Sometimes the saga has a happy ending and sometimes not. In some cases, the sheds are found years later, or perhaps only one side of the rack is found, never to be matched up. The journey can be filled with heartaches and extreme highs.

I'm not sure which is easier: trying to kill a trophy buck or trying to find the sheds from one. Both have their challenges. Another hunter could kill your trophy, or it could be hit by a car. When hunting, you're restricted by season length and bag limits. However, a mature deer moving through the woods is much easier to spot than an antler lying idly on the forest floor, so I'd tend to say shed hunting is more difficult.

Some shed hunters accumulate several antlers from the same buck over the years, either because they're lucky shed hunters or unlucky deer hunters. Putting together several years' worth of matched sets off the same buck would be the shed-hunting equivalent to hitting a grand slam. However, finding several years' worth of matched sets and eventually killing the deer would be the ultimate challenge.

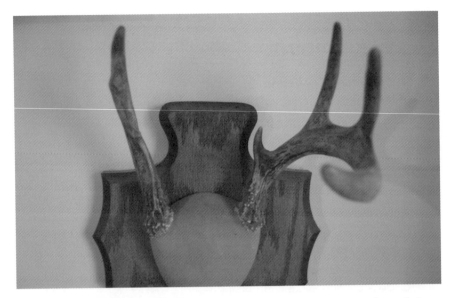

Determining whether two antlers are a match isn't always easy. As the rack from this buck -- killed by the author's hunting partner Ryan Bybee -- shows, matching antlers aren't always mirror images.

If you're fortunate enough to capture scouting-camera photos of bucks in your area, accurately matching up sets of antlers becomes much easier.

STICKER POINT:

Not a Match: Case in Point

A pair of 4-point sheds from a northern Minnesota deer yard illustrates the differences that otherwise similar-looking antlers may possess. I found both sheds on the same day about 300 yards apart. Both were from that spring, although one had been on the ground much longer, judging by its lack of a skin ring and some staining where the antler contacted the ground. One antler was a right side and one was a left side, and each carried four points with the same configuration, and they scored within an inch of each other when measured. So far, it sounds like a possible match, right? However, the left antler is very dark between the base and brow tine, and the right is lighter in color. That fact alone would indicate the sheds are not a match because the coloration comes from rubbing, and obviously both antlers would have to be colored the same. But wait, there's more. The left antler's main beam is significantly shorter vertically, that is, it bends sooner than the right antler's. The left side also carries more mass. The right antler sits taller and has longer tines but less mass. The final clue that proves these sheds are not from the same buck is the fact that when held together like they would sit on a skull, they don't sit at the same angle and just don't look right.

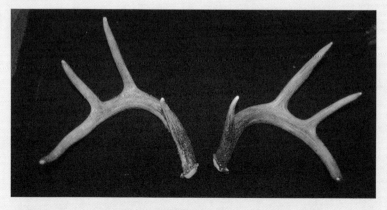

Despite the close proximity of these antlers and their similar appearance, several elements prove that these sheds from a Minnesota deer yard are not a match.

STICKER POINT:

That First Matched Set

I'll never forget my first matched set; probably no shed addict ever does. I was searching some new grounds just a couple miles from home. I didn't hold much stock in the area, considering it was public hunting land consisting of a big swamp with very little agriculture in the area. The swamp was so vast that it seemed finding sheds would be out of the question. Well, that soupy swamp must have turned off most hunters, too, because I soon learned there were bucks everywhere. On my second trip into the area, I was just about to give up my search for the day when I found a 2-point right side. The next day I returned, eager to find more antlers. As I walked into the swamp, a white object poking up caught my eye. Was it an antler? I couldn't tell, but my motto is "when in doubt, check it out," so I did. When I was 10 yards from the object in question, I was pretty sure it was just a stick, but as I walked closer, I nearly stepped on an actual antler, and 3 feet from it was another shed! It was my first matched set … or so I thought. The white object that had originally caught my eye was actually a stick, but if I hadn't stopped to check it out, I'd have never seen the pair of antlers. I left the sheds where they lay, hung my hat in a tree and raced back to my truck for my camera. Granted, the antlers were just small sheds, but if you'd have seen me flying through the woods, feet barely hitting the ground in my haste, you'd have thought I'd have found the sheds to the next world record whitetail. I snapped photos of the antlers where they lay, but only after I picked up the 2-point left side and 3-point right side did I realize they weren't a match! However, the 2-point left side was the match to the antler I'd found the day before, and the following year I found the match to the 3-point side. I went from a high of thinking I'd found a matched set, to a low of realizing I hadn't, to an extreme high of finding two matched sets!

Lessons in Bone

Shed hunting is much more than just a walk in the woods; it can be a serious scouting tool for deer hunters. Matching up a set of sheds hundreds of yards apart gives you an idea of how deer move through the woods, but there's much more to it than that. Shed hunting teaches us which trails deer walk, the foods they eat and even their general health. At the very least, finding a shed is evidence of which bucks have survived the hunting season and are wintering in your area. Keep in mind, however, that in northern areas where deer migrate to winter habitat, the deer that drop sheds in one area may be miles away by hunting season (although they may return while late-season muzzleloader or archery hunts are still open). But in more southern areas, deer are found in the same general area year-round. Here's how you can glean the most information from the sheds you find.

Perhaps the most valuable aspect of shed hunting is the fact that you can thoroughly scout an area without the least concern over bumping deer. So often during pre-season or in-season scouting trips, deer hunters are almost afraid to set foot in the woods for fear of spooking deer, which could cause them to vacate the area or move less frequently during daylight. However, when you're shed hunting in late winter or early spring, jumping deer shouldn't be a concern. Deer will have months to return to their preferred bedding and feeding areas. This unabashed approach to shed hunting and scouting gives you a chance to really get in there, scout a property and learn every inch of it, rather than finding sign, hanging a stand and backing out before you get a real feel for the big picture.

Health Indices

We can learn a lot about the health of the deer herd by studying antlers. Simply observing when deer shed their antlers can tell you something about the health of a deer. If you learn that the buck shed its antlers late in the winter, either by observation or from finding bloody (freshly shed) antlers, you can assume the deer was in good health. Poor health, either from poor nutrition or stress, causes deer to shed their antlers early. When using shedding date as a health index, make sure you're comparing deer from your region. Average shedding date varies by latitude and even somewhat by habitat type.

Scientists have found correlations between an antler's physical nature and the health of the individual buck that carried it. As mentioned in Chapter 1, testosterone levels play a major role in the growth and casting of antlers.

Bubenik and Schams graphed a correlation between testosterone levels and antler seal depth. (The seal is the very bottom of a shed, which connects to the buck's head.) The scientists found bucks with higher testosterone levels (and presumably greater antler-growing potential) had convex seals, while those with the lowest testosterone levels had concave seals.

The beam diameter of shed antlers can also give you a clue as to the health of the deer herd – both bucks and does. Studies have shown that the average beam diameter of yearling bucks in a given area is a good indicator of a given deer's body weight. In other words, the greater the average beam diameter, the larger the

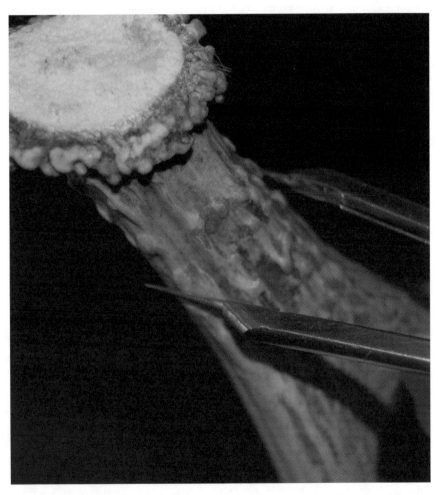

Yearling buck antler beam diameter can be used as a guide to determine the buck's health, and it can be further extrapolated to doe health as well.

body weight and the healthier the deer. Researchers measure beam diameter ½ to 1 inch above the burr using a fine caliper to avoid measuring knobs of beading along the beam that would distort the measurement. Likewise, beam diameter has been linked to fawn production. Simply put, where ample food is available for the entire herd, bucks will grow larger antlers and does will produce more and healthier fawns. Be forewarned, however, that average yearling buck beam diameter varies regionally, and even on different habitat types within a state. In order to accurately assess the health of the deer herd in your area based on beam diameter, you'll have to check with a local biologist to determine whether beam-diameter measurements have been studied in your region. You could also keep detailed records of the antlers you find on your own hunting grounds from year to year to trace health trends in your local deer herd.

As mentioned, these beam-diameter studies measure antlers from yearling bucks, which are generally sampled at hunter registration stations where biologists can efficiently obtain a large sample size. Also, because the entire field-dressed carcass is available, biologists can decisively determine the deer's age based on tooth examination. Although a yearling buck antler is generally easy to identify as such, when you're shed hunting, the luxury of tooth sampling is not available, and therefore, there is a shadow of doubt cast over the identification of any "yearling buck" antlers you find. Although most yearling antlers are generally characterized by their small size and small base diameter, keep in mind there is no way to be sure the shed antler you are examining didn't come from a malnourished or genetically inferior older deer. As such, you should use your assessment only as a general indication of herd health.

Another way to measure the health of the bucks in your area would be to note the occurrence of spike bucks in the herd. As a general rule, the more spikes in the herd, the worse the health of the deer. Bucks that grow branched antlers as yearlings (2 points per side or more) can generally be considered in good health. The only problem with using the presence of spike bucks as an indicator of herd health is that, simply put, spike buck sheds are very difficult to find. In essence, the shed hunter who is lucky enough to find a spike shed antler actually isn't that lucky after all, for the deer that grew it may be malnourished or have inferior genetics.

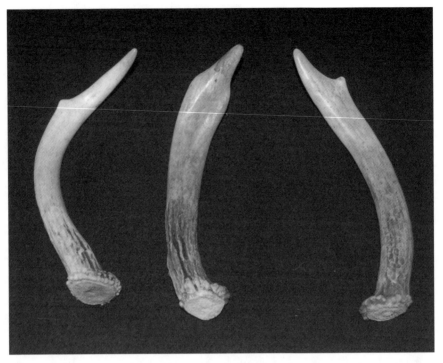

The presence of many spike bucks in a deer herd may indicate poor herd health. However, due to their small size, finding spike antlers isn't easy.

The Finer Points

The more time you spend in deer habitat, the more you learn about deer. I can honestly say I learn more about deer from shed hunting than from books, magazines, videos or even my time spent hunting. The reasons are simple. First, when I'm shed hunting, I'm not worried about spooking deer, so I feel free to follow a rub line, amble down a deer trail or kneel by a scrape for detailed study. Second, when you're trying to find an antler, or especially when you're trying to match up a rack, you've got to pay attention to details. You must be a detective and follow every clue that could lead you to the whereabouts of antlers. It's something that hunters should do all the time, but again in our haste to leave an area before we disturb it, we sometimes gloss over subtle deer signs. Walking slowly through the woods and staring at the ground can reveal some surprising things about deer behavior.

One thing that shed hunting taught me, which might have taken me a long time to discover without taking long walks in the spring woods, is how frequently deer utilize open areas. It's popular belief that bucks reside in thick protective cover to avoid detection by predators, but this isn't always true. In winter, deer often bed on the north edge of a forest opening. The northern edge, just like the southern slope of a hill, receives the most direct sunlight in winter, which melts snow here first and warms the air slightly more than the surrounding air. From this position, deer can also monitor winter winds prevailing from the north for predators and keep tabs on other deer.

Antlers can also give you clues as to where bucks hang out, which is especially helpful after you've found a shed and are looking for the match, or whether you're simply trying to unravel travel patterns. Are there pieces of bark in the burrs? Does the antler feel sticky or smell like pine? If you can identify the trees the buck has been rubbing, you may be able to unravel a travel pattern and narrow your search for the match. Also note antler color. I've found sheds that vary from chocolate brown to bone white, and everything in between. Old antlers that are a year old or more will be bone white because the sun bleaches them, but sometimes fresh antlers are white, too. Think back to how many times you've seen a buck with white antlers, either in the wild or in photos. Most likely that buck lives in open range with few trees and the sun bleaches the antlers while they're still on the buck's head. In fact, I've found bone-white antlers with bloody bases, so they were obviously freshly shed. If you're finding fresh white sheds in a wooded area, especially when you're finding other darker-colored antlers in the same area, chances are the buck is spending a lot of time in forest clearings or even out in a grassland. You can use this knowledge in future shed-hunting trips and during hunting season.

Finding sheds (or not finding them) can also reveal changes to deer habitat and movements. One year I found several sheds in a thick conifer swamp. After learning the property that spring and seeing a large buck that eluded me twice that fall, I was excited for my shed-hunting prospects the following year. However, the following spring I scoured the property the best I could and came up with a single year-old shed. What happened? In situations like this, if you feel you put in a consistent shed hunting effort from one year to the next, you can conclude that something changed. Maybe crops were rotated, land was developed or hunting pressure was higher that year. In my case, an extensive clear-cut was conducted about a half-mile away. The slash would have provided food and cover for deer, and I believe they simply shifted their wintering area accordingly.

STICKER POINT:

Elementary, My Dear Watson

In a lot of ways, shed hunters are like detectives. We are trying to unravel the mystery of where fallen antlers may be lying. The best shed hunters use every clue available to help them solve the puzzle. Scouting while bucks are still carrying their antlers is a critical component to shed-hunting success, but what about after antlers drop? Be savvy and let the antlers themselves tell you how and where to hunt for them. If you're finding lots of old antlers but cannot, despite your best efforts, find fresh sheds, a couple scenarios may have happened. For one thing, someone could have come through and scooped up all the freshies and left the old ones lay. But more likely, deer may have switched their wintering area. Scout around within a few hundred yards or perhaps a mile or two away and you may be into the fresh sheds.

Antlers can also give you clues as to where bucks hang out, which is especially helpful after you've found a shed and are looking for the match. Are there pieces of bark in the burrs? Does the antler feel sticky or smell like pine? If you can identify the trees the buck has been rubbing, you may be able to narrow your search for the match. Also note antler color. If the shed is bone white on just one side, it may have been lying on the ground for a while, but if the shed is fresh and the entire antler is bone white, you can assume that buck has been spending a lot of time in the open where the sun has bleached his antler while still atop his head. Skip the woods and head for the open ground to find the match.

Keeping a Shed-Hunting Journal

Call me an extremist, but I admit that I keep a journal of all my sheds. I've always kept fishing and hunting journals, and I'm amazed at the patterns I figure out by comparing the data in them from year to year. Shed journals do the same thing, so record the details of your find as soon as you discover it.

Recording all your finds in a journal will help you learn more about deer and unravel patterns in your area.

In my journal, I note the following pieces of information:

- Date each antler was found
- Where I found it (both the property and the specific location, such as "south edge of red pine plantation at paper company land")
- Whether it was old or new
- The antler's orientation (Was it tines up or down? What did I see first that tipped me off?) and lastly,
- How I think it fell off (Was the deer walking, feeding, bedding, jumping, rubbing?)

Here's an example: "March 8: Found two fresh sheds from different bucks 15 yards apart at Mike's place. There is a strip of tall white pines that lie at the edge of the swamp, right along a picked cornfield. I figured the pines would be a good place to bed because they block the wind, and under the trees is the only place in the general area where the ground is bare of snow. First antler was tines down under a big pine, and the second was tines up, also under a pine. The bucks must have been bedded there."

Journal entries tell me a number of things. First, the date tells me a lot. If I find a fresh antler on February 5, I can assume that other bucks in the area have dropped by this date as well. However, if I find an old antler in a favorite spot that I check every year, and I can look back at my shed journal and see that my last trip to that area was March 18 of the previous year, I might have simply missed it last year, or maybe the buck hadn't shed as of March 18 last year. Maybe in future seasons it would be wise to search this area later in the year.

The other information, such as the antler's orientation and how I think it fell off help me know what to look for when I'm shed hunting. Over time I can look at my journal and reaffirm that seeing the antler base is something that really stands out for me and helps me identify the object as an antler, not a limb.

In addition to recording your antler finds in a journal, an as-it-lay photo will help you remember the details.

STICKER POINT:

Being in the Zone

There are two basic parts of shed hunting: scouting and execution. Scouting consists of finding where the deer are, whether that means finding a piece of ground where bucks are protected from hunting or whether you have to observe migrating whitetails to see where they winter. Once you've found the best place to shed hunt, you have to get out there and pick up antlers, which isn't always easy.

Athletes often talk about being "in the zone." When athletes are in the zone, they are so focused and in tune with what they're doing that the mind and body function as one well-oiled unit. A baseball player may see the ball come off the pitcher's hand and watch it spinning seemingly in slow motion all the way to the plate. The batter's eyes relay the vision to the brain, and the brain orders the arms to swing the bat, driving the ball out of the ballpark, seemingly without effort. If you've ever felt this feeling, you know what I'm talking about.

The best shed hunters put themselves in a similar state of mind. Your attention should be focused on unraveling a deer's travel pattern and looking for pieces of antler – not the office, your family and what you're having for supper. Don't get distracted. If you see a deer or a bird that catches your eye, by all means, take a look – after all, there's more to shed hunting than just finding antlers. But when you divert your attention away from the ground, stop first and resume shed hunting only when you've re-focused. It's so easy to follow the flight of that first robin of spring, only to realize you don't remember what the ground looked like for the last 50 yards. The bottom line is when you're shed hunting, you're shed hunting. Conversations, relaxation and enjoying nature are all part of shed hunting, but don't let these activities become your primary focus. Sometimes, when you're really into it, you'll get in an area that looks so good that you seemingly know when you're about to find a shed. You may think to yourself, "This looks really good. I'm going to find one right here," and boom, a shed appears. Don't laugh – it happens! When you're calling sheds before you find them, you know you're really in the shed-hunting zone!

Making an educated guess as to how the antler dropped helps me establish patterns. I might be able to conclude that a lot of deer in a given area drop their antlers along the south-facing edge of a woodlot as they travel between their bedding and feeding area in a given spot. This helps me concentrate my efforts in the most productive areas. Having the shed's location is also helpful, because it's not unusual for a particular buck to drop its antlers in the same spot each year, sometimes within feet of the previous year's sheds. You might even consider carrying a GPS unit with you on your shed hunts so you can punch in the exact location where you find an antler for future reference in finding the matching antler or subsequent sheds. Also, because bucks often travel in bachelor groups in winter, there's a good chance that other bucks could be in the area. Usually if I find one antler on a shed outing, I find another in the same general area, and quite often, it's from an entirely different buck. Also, deer tend to use the same

Label each shed you find so you can match it with its corresponding journal entry. A simple tag tied to the antler works well and won't ruin the shed.

wintering areas from year to year, so a spot that is productive one year should be equally productive the next. The bottom line is, if I find an antler, I make it a point to search the area diligently, and check the same spot in subsequent years, and the only way for me to remember all the details is to keep a shed journal.

You can obviously learn a lot from the sheds you accumulate by keeping a shed journal, but all this information loses its impact if you can't correspond it with your sheds. For this reason, you should label your antlers. My labeling system simply involves writing a number on a cardboard tag tied to the antler. The number corresponds to an entry in my shed journal. If journaling isn't your thing but you still want to organize your antler data, you could just scribble information on the card, such as date found, location and other relevant details. Many people write information on their sheds with permanent marker. This certainly ensures that you'll remember when and where you found a particular antler, but think twice before you write on a shed. You may regret it later.

6
Alternative Methods

S ore feet and eye strain isn't the only recipe for finding antlers. It's human nature to look for an easier way to do something, and shed hunting is no different. Some of these "shortcut" methods are more effective than others, but you may want to consider them to help put more antlers in your hands.

The easiest trick is to simply give your feet a rest and hop in a truck or on a snowmobile, ATV, tractor or horse. Obviously this method has its limitations; you can't go cruising through a brushy bedding area on an ATV, but in open terrain, this method works well. Feeding areas, particularly low-cut soybean stubble or alfalfa fields, are ideally suited to this method because they are both attractive to deer in winter and provide excellent visibility. Riding a horse, snowmobile, ATV, truck or tractor also lets you cover a lot of ground quickly from a higher vantage point, further improving your vision. It may also be helpful to have a passenger along who can devote full attention to searching, and not driving. Be forewarned, however, that fields are usually soft and muddy in spring, and the landowner may not appreciate you rutting up a field ... or a knock on his door when you get stuck.

ATVs can help you cover ground faster and more efficiently, while giving your feet much-needed rest.

Winter deer feeding is a popular activity, particularly in the north, where heavy snow cover makes finding food difficult for deer, and on southern ranches where deer are commonly fed year-round. Deer also regularly visit backyard feeders throughout the winter, and it's not surprising that they often leave antlers behind. Some folks who regularly feed deer opt to help the shedding process along by incorporating antler-stripping devices into their feeders. These consist of anything from simple stakes arranged around the food to elaborate chicken-wire contraptions. Commercially made products consisting essentially of an array of bungee cords around a 5-gallon bucket are also available. These devices may sound like an ingenious idea, however, antler strippers have their drawbacks. For one thing, if a buck isn't physically ready to cast its antlers, no device is going to knock them off. Then, a buck could destroy the feeder as it struggles to free its antlers, or worse, its antlers might become entangled in the feeder, causing undue stress to a winter-weary whitetail. With this knowledge in mind, use a bit of common sense and caution if you plan to use antler strippers.

Attracting Deer With Food Plots

One method that can brings sheds to you, rather than vice versa, is to plant a food plot. If the plot is attractive to deer in winter, with a little luck, in spring you may find a few antlers in your plot. But finding sheds isn't as easy as planting seed and harvesting a crop of sheds; there is much more to consider.

Spring plantings can attract deer the following winter at shedding time. However, keep in mind that deer may begin using these plots in summer, through fall and into winter as long as a crop is still available. For this reason, it's imperative to plant large food plots. Deer will quickly devour small, irregularly shaped plots designed for hunting. Depending on the deer density in your area and what other food sources are available, food plots ranging from 2 to 5 acres in size will be better shed producers, simply because it's more likely that food will still be available in winter in these larger food plots.

Fall plantings are an option, but growing them can be an uphill battle. Most plant species need at least 45 days to reach maturity, and some species, such as corn, take considerably longer to grow. The first frost will stop or slow the growth of most crops. As a result, your fall plot will yield far less tonnage than the same plot planted in the spring. Fall plots may be a bit more appealing to shed seekers south of the snowbelt, as crops can grow later into the winter months, but even throughout many areas of the south, frosts can wreak havoc on food plots.

Deer will dig through deep snow to reach preferred food sources.

If you've decided that food plots are at least worth a shot as a shed-hunting tool, what should you plant? Brassica is a top choice for a few reasons. If planted in spring, it will yield far more tonnage than a fall planting, and best of all, deer tend to ignore the crop in summer, allowing it to reach its maximum yield without being browsed back. Plus, in the fall, after the first frost or two, the bitter-tasting plant's starches are chemically converted to sugars, which makes the now-sweet-tasting plant much more appealing to deer. Deer will continue to browse brassica far into the winter until the crop is depleted.

Another food plot option is corn. The love affair deer have with corn is no secret to farmland deer hunters or farmers. The only problem with corn shed-hunting plots is getting the crop to last past the fall and into the shedding months. Deer, as well as raccoons, squirrels and even birds will work away at the golden ears, devouring it in short order in small plots. If you can plant a large enough corn plot to keep deer coming into the winter months, you'll have an excellent chance of finding sheds come spring. Not only do deer favor eating corn, but the crop's high carbohydrate content can keep deer going in cold winters.

Teaching a dog a new trick? With a little training, you can teach a dog to use its nose to sniff out antlers. Photo by Doug Coleman.

Rye grass is another plant that draws deer in winter, and at least one shed hunter I know always keeps his eyes open for food plots and farm fields planted to rye grass. This crop can be planted in fall and is a bit more tolerant of cold weather. It will continue growing after a few mild frosts. It is highly attractive to deer in winter, although it's not necessarily the best winter deer food.

There are many more food plot choices, but these are probably your best bets. Others, like chicory and the ever-popular clover go dormant in winter and are less attractive to deer. But with that said, keep in mind that survival is paramount to deer in winter and they'll utilize whatever foods are available. In fact, I've seen clover food plots buried under a foot of snow torn up as if a pack of wild dogs was looking for a buried bone under the snow. In reality, these huge excavations were created by deer hoofs, and the entire plot was riddled with these diggings, as well as beds and tracks. These deer were after the same clover they'd been feeding on that fall and weren't about to let 12 inches of snow keep them from it.

If you're already growing food plots on your land, note which ones have produced sheds in the past. If not, talk to other landowners in your area and see which crops have worked the best for them. For more detailed information on food plots, contact your county extension office.

Shed Dogs

As shed hunting has grown more popular in recent years, some serious shed-seekers have turned to man's best friend to help them tally more sheds. If dogs could be trained to hunt birds, detect drugs and sniff out bombs, why couldn't they be trained to find shed antlers?

The truth is, they can, and in fact, dogs can be quite effective shed hunters. It's well known that a dog's sense of smell is far superior to our own, and thusly, dogs find antlers by scent as well as sight. In fact, many are the story where a shed hunter spotted an antler, sent a dog to retrieve it, and was surprised when the dog suddenly veered off after apparently catching the right scent and retrieved the matching antler instead.

Nearly any type of dog can be taught to find antlers, but the retrieving types, such as Labs, Chesapeakes, golden retrievers and the like are most suitable because they are natural retrievers and have a desire to please their owners. A more important consideration than breed is the individual dog's motivation to find antlers. Simply put, if the dog shows little interest in retrieving sheds, or soon grows bored with the activity, it won't make a great shed dog.

Some trainers now teach dogs specifically to find antlers. Tracy Bowling, of Ventosa Kennel in Scotland Neck, N.C., (www.ventosakennel.com) may be one of the best-known. If you're looking for a serious shed-hunting dog, he will train your dog if it has the right capabilities, or you can buy a trained dog from him. Tracy also offers courses that will teach you how to train your own shed-hunting dog at home. I won't pretend to be a dog-training expert, but here are some tips to help you train your own dog to find antlers.

Begin with the basics. Teach your dog the routine obedience commands of sit, stay and heel. You can't expect a dog to mind you when exploring the distracting sights and smells of the spring woods if it won't simply sit when told.

Start your dog early. You know how the old saying goes: you can't teach an old dog new tricks. Many shed dog owners get a dog acquainted with antlers the same day they bring them home from the kennel. They're not expecting the dog to find antlers buried under a foot of snow at 8 weeks, but they do like to let the dog smell the antler and maybe get a feel for it in its mouth. It's a good idea to round off any pointed tines on a training antler so the dog doesn't hurt itself either when chewing on it or when running with it.

Work with your dog. Professional athletes don't develop their athletic talents overnight without training, so don't expect great things from your dog if you can't spend time training it. A few short sessions each week will teach and develop a dog better than an intensive training session once a month.

Round 'em up, Cowboy!

If there could be a shed dog celebrity, it would be Cowboy, a black lab owned by Doug and Tammy Coleman of Idaho. Cowboy has his own entries accepted in the North American Shed Hunters Club record book. He also stars in three shed-hunting videos the Colemans have produced called Through the Eyes of a Shed Hunter, volumes I, II and III.

Tammy's efforts training Cowboy have made shed hunts much more productive and enjoyable for the Colemans. Tammy used a simple, but effective, technique to train Cowboy. When he was a puppy, she immediately rewarded him with a treat each time he followed his basic obedience commands. Tammy worked with him two or three times a week for about an hour to get Cowboy interested in sheds. Cowboy loves to fetch balls, but when Tammy began to get serious with his shed training, she rewarded him with a treat only when he brought back an antler.

Cowboy takes a break to show off a recent find. Photo by Doug Coleman.

Canada may be Mecca for shed hunters. Plentiful deer numbers and low hunting pressure in the prairie provinces can yield outstanding shed hunting.

When Cowboy got a little older, Tammy started taking him out of the yard for in-field training. She would hide antlers in a grassy field for Cowboy to find, but it quickly became apparent he was simply following her scent trail right to the antlers. So Tammy began throwing them. This forced Cowboy to use his nose to circle around until he caught the scent of an antler.

When Cowboy began accompanying the Colemans on actual shed hunts, Doug and Tammy would call him when they found a shed. (At least if the antler was small. If it was a large shed, like most everyone, they couldn't help themselves and ran to it!) Once they'd found a shed, they told Cowboy to 'find a horn.' With some encouragement and some circling, he was able to find these sheds too, which of course, had no human scent on them.

Soon, Cowboy began to get the idea. Although he does often stick tight to the couple, he has learned to range back and forth between them and cover more ground. The Colemans often walk the edges of thick cover and let Cowboy cover the thick tangles in between.

For whatever reason, Cowboy can distinguish between antlers and other bones, and only brings back sheds. And, after all these years, he is still immediately rewarded with a treat for every antler he finds.

Out-of-state shed hunts can put you in new territory, where different deer species live. The author picked up this beautiful matched set of mule deer antlers in Saskatchewan.

Doug and Tammy are constantly amazed at how Cowboy reacts to antler scents. Sometimes Cowboy walks right past freshly shed antlers lying mere feet away. Sometimes the wind just doesn't seem to be in his favor. However, quite often Cowboy is a shed magnet, sniffing out antlers the Colemans would otherwise never find. Doug related a time when Cowboy was walking toward the couple when he locked up so abruptly he nearly fell over. He dove into the grass and discovered a year-old shed that was buried under the grass. Doug is still amazed by that find.

For the Colemans, Cowboy is a great companion and a real help when it comes to finding antlers. They almost wouldn't dream of going shed hunting without him. To see Cowboy in action, and to see great footage of shed hunting for whitetail, mule deer and elk sheds in the *Through the Eyes of a Shed Hunter* video series, e-mail the Colemans at dtcoleman@cableone.net.

Guided Shed Hunts

In recent years, as shed hunting has grown more popular, serious shed seekers have looked for better ways to locate more and bigger sheds. One radical new concept was this: if deer hunters could book out-of-state hunts, why couldn't shed hunters? The guided shed hunt was born.

Although guided shed hunts are still in their infancy, the number of outfitters who offer them is growing each year. Most shed hunts are offered in Canada, although a few U.S. outfitters have moved into the market.

Each guided shed hunt is unique in the way it's conducted, often depending on the type of habitat where you'll be walking. You may be searching in hardwoods and food plots in Illinois, CRP fields in Kansas, buck brush and aspen stands in Saskatchewan or an island in the lake country of Ontario.

In addition, you may find more antlers during a few days on a guided trip than you would in an entire season at home. Plus, depending on where you go, you may be able to find sheds from mule deer, elk or moose in addition to whitetails.

Aside from booking shed hunts as a way for finding large sheds, a high volume of antlers or sheds from other species, there are other reasons for doing so. The most popular is to get acquainted with the landscape where you'll be booking a deer hunt in the fall. Some guides offer spring shed hunts at reduced rates to clients who book fall deer hunts with them. Shed hunting in spring gives hunters a chance to become familiar with the area they'll be hunting without fear of spooking deer. Some outfitters will even let you choose your own fall stand sites based on your spring scouting.

Shed hunting in the spring gives clients an opportunity to observe deer sign left from the winter and unravel deer patterns and movements. Best of all, it gives them an opportunity to learn what caliber of deer they'll be hunting in fall. In fact, if they're extremely lucky, they might be fortunate enough to find a buck's sheds in the spring and tag the deer during hunting season.

Prices vary, but a guided shed hunt typically runs about $250 per day, with lodging and meals included. The rules of booking a shed hunt are the same as those governing a guided deer hunt. If you want a quality experience, go with an outfitter with a solid reputation. Ask for a list of references, and ask past clients about the hospitality, hidden costs, the guide's personality, the number and quality of sheds found and the overall shed-hunting experience.

Ask about the terrain in the area where you'll be shedding. Find out whether it's open or wooded, and if you need any special clothing, such as hip boots, brush pants or heavy winter clothing. Pack accordingly and bring plenty of socks and extra footwear in case your boots get wet. Also bring along items to care for your feet, such as bandages, antibiotic ointment, etc.

It's also a good idea to ask the outfitter how many shed hunters he guides each year and how much area he has to roam. If it's public land, how much competition is there from other shed hunters, both locals and clients of other guides? Will you have plenty of fresh ground to cover? Find out what time of year is best in the outfitter's area. Book too early and you may have snow to contend with, but a trip too late in the year may have you fighting your way through a green jungle. In Canada, it's often best to book a trip late to make sure the snow has melted. There are relatively few rodents in Canada, especially in the pasturelands of Saskatchewan and Alberta, so chewed antlers aren't usually a problem.

Ask your guide to fill you in on all the details before you depart for your trip. If you're flying, will the guide pick you up at the airport? Will someone be with you in the field or will you just be dropped off with a few simple instructions? Are food and lodging included? What is a typical day of shed hunting like? Will you be on foot or riding an ATV? Find out if lunch and snacks are provided. You'll need plenty of energy if you're going to be walking for up to 10 hours a day.

In short, do your homework so your booked shed hunt is memorable for all the right reasons.

Canadian Red Tape

One of the biggest considerations if you're shed hunting in Canada is getting your antlers home. As of this writing, U.S. residents are limited in the number of antlers they can bring across the border from Canada. The transport restrictions stem from concerns of introducing diseases, such as bovine spongiform encephalopathies, into the United States. On top of this, the rules governing how many antlers you can bring into the United States is subject to the interpretation of the specific point of entry, and perhaps even the border control agent on duty that day. After speaking with numerous border-control agents, as well as many confused shed hunters, I've found trying to get absolute answers on the exact import process is maddening. Most ports of entry will allow you to bring two matched sets (four antlers) with you across the border without any special permits. More lax entry points will allow you to bring any four sheds, (not necessarily matched sets) as long as they are free of dirt, blood and other animal tissue. Because these rules are so variable, you MUST plan ahead! A few weeks before your trip, contact the exact port of entry you'll be using. Tell them your plans and ask what the regulations are. Then, most importantly, get the agent's name and contact number for future reference. For a list of ports of entry, visit www.customs.gov.

Because most shed hunters will (hopefully) be bringing back more than just four sheds, the safest plan, in addition to taking the above precautions, is to acquire an import/export permit. It allows you to bring back multiple antlers … with just a little red tape. You'll need the Federal Fish and Wildlife License/ Permit Application Form (Form 3-200-3). You can download the application at www.fws.gov/forms/3-200-3.pdf. This permit lasts for one year and is renewable. The current cost is $100. Plan ahead because this permit may take up to 90 days to process.

In addition to the U.S. Fish and Wildlife Service permit listed above, you'll need the Veterinary Health Certificate of Export of Cervid Antlers to the United States. This is form HA2300, available from the Canadian government. Once you've found sheds and are planning a return trip to the United States, you must have an official veterinarian from the Canadian Food Inspection Agency examine your antlers. The veterinarian will certify that the antlers are "clean, dry, and free of soil, clay, tissue, and dried pieces of hide, flesh, sinew and other related materials." Upon satisfactory examination, the veterinarian will sign the document and provide an official export stamp. For more information visit www.inspection.gc.ca

These are the current regulations. They are constantly changing, and again, subject to interpretation. Please call your specific point of entry prior to your trip to make sure your return to the United States goes smoothly. The last thing you want is to be holding your shed of a lifetime in front of a border-control agent who is giving you the headache of a lifetime. It should be noted that nonresidents are not allowed to shed hunt in Manitoba.

As another word of caution to travelers to Canada, be aware that border regulations have changed. As of Dec. 31, 2006, passengers flying in and out of Canada from the United States must have a passport, instead of a birth certificate. The same rule takes effect for all land border crossings on Dec. 31, 2007.

STICKER POINT:

A Canadian Shed Hunt

I booked my first shed-hunting trip with Bentley Coben of Tessier, Saskatchewan. Bentley has found more than 1,000 whitetail and mule deer sheds measuring at least 60 inches, and he's been guiding shed hunters for more than a decade. His house is a virtual antler museum!

Bentley scouts for deer all winter and knows where the best shedding grounds will be, even if deer shift their habitat slightly from year to year. There are large bucks in his area, several of which would qualify for the Boone & Crockett record book. There are thousands of acres of public land in the area that offer top-notch shed hunting, and you never need to worry about covering picked-over ground. Plus, Bentley generously sacrifices his own time afield to put his clients in his best shedding grounds, often returning to the truck with fewer sheds than his guests.

A typical day on that trip consisted of about 10 hours of walking through open pasture and aspen stands and glassing from rolling foothills. I found both whitetail and mule deer sheds, but although there was plenty of moose sign, I couldn't come up with a moose paddle.

Bentley's wife, Dianne, is a fantastic cook and wouldn't let me leave the table, even when I couldn't possibly eat another bite. There were no concerns of being hungry, even when afield most of the day. Plus, the Cobens are some of the most genuine and hospitable folks you'll ever meet and I left feeling I had made new friends.

During my three-day shed hunt I found 43 antlers, including a 7-point whitetail shed that measured 78 inches and a matched set of drop-tine mule deer sheds measuring 74 and 80 inches, which were the first two mulie sheds I ever found! On the first day alone Bentley's guide, Shane, and I found 50 sheds between the two of us, and at one point I picked up 14 in an hour. I wish it was always that easy.

I found more sheds in those three days than I usually find in a couple of years of searching the public lands of Wisconsin, and most of the sheds were from bucks aged 2½ or older. I can't wait to go back!

For more information, contact Bentley Coben at (306) 656-4903 or www.BentleyCoben.com.

Fragmented forests pose unique challenges for urban shed hunters.

Shedding in the 'Burbs

Deer hunters often fantasize about legendary bucks that live deep in thick, dark swamps where they grow record-book racks and survive for a decade without seeing a human. As a deer hunter, I'd like to think there are still places where these swamp legends lurk. But in today's world, some of the truly impressive bucks don't live miles away in impenetrable cover. In fact, they may literally be living in your own back yard.

One of the most amazing things about white-tailed deer – and there are many – is their ability to adapt to different habitat types. They thrive in forests, grasslands, marshes and mountains. And today, they frequent back yards, city parks and suburban nature centers.

Shed hunting in the suburbs can be nothing short of fantastic, and folks who know where to look can come up with 100 or more sheds a year because of high deer densities and lack of hunting pressure. But like anything with a high potential payoff, there are also some serious drawbacks to suburban shed hunting – namely competition. In areas of such high human populations, big bucks don't fly under the radar. Many folks may be trying to pattern the same bucks to score their sheds, and competition among shed hunters in the suburbs can border on the ridiculous. In some areas, shed hunters are almost forced to hit the woods every day to pick up fresh sheds before someone else does.

The other hard reality of urban shed hunting is access. Although you might have a good sense of the locations bucks frequent, it may be next to impossible to access private lots that deer use. Also, shed hunting is often off-limits in the nature preserves and parks that shelter suburban deer. Still, the payoffs are there, especially considering bucks in more urban areas are protected from hunting, and thus, can live to maturity and reach their full antler-growing potential.

It's a universal truth that deer need food and shelter wherever they are found, and suburban deer are no exception. But these deer may have much smaller home ranges, simply because they are more limited in the amount of food and cover available. As a result, it may be easier to pinpoint their movements, but not necessarily find their sheds, once again because of competition and access. Deer in the 'burbs aren't shy, and they'll bed wherever they can find suitable habitat, be it a wooded residential lot, city park, gravel pit, forest preserve or stream corridor. Because of a suburban area's fragmented nature, deer often have well-defined travel corridors that will reveal their movements.

It's not unusual for people to find sheds in their yards, especially for those residing adjacent to large blocks of forested cover. Deer often bed in heavy cover during the day and enter residential yards at night, where they feed on gardens, ornamental plants and shrubs and spilled seed from bird feeders. However, unless you live in such a lot, gaining access probably isn't a strong possibility.

As cities grow, land on the outskirts of town is prone to development, and farms that once seemed quaint just at the edge of town are being enveloped. Pressure to sell and million-dollar offers frequently cause farmers to sell off their lands to developers. However, if you can gain shed-hunting access from a stalwart farmer still clinging to his land at city's edge, the shed hunting can be phenomenal.

As mentioned, other places to try include forest preserves, city parks, nature centers and other government lands. Some are regulated against collecting natural artifacts – including sheds – while others are not. Check with city ordinances, local wildlife agencies or nature preserve centers for more information. Privately owned commercial lands can also harbor large concentrations of deer. Golf courses, quarries, gravel pits and office buildings with wooded acreage come to mind. It never hurts to ask for access to these places.

As always, observe where you routinely observe deer and be creative. Especially in urban areas, some of the best places can be small, overlooked areas that others pass by. And when you find a good spot, be tight-lipped about it.

No matter where you begin your search, remember that urban deer may behave somewhat differently than wild deer. Deer are often much more accustomed to human encounters, and I'm constantly amazed at how often huge bucks will bed near houses and busy streets. Deer are simply more tolerant of human activity in areas of higher human populations, so keep that in mind while you're walking.

7
Competition and the
Shed-Hunting Community

Problems With Finding Antlers

After a long, hard-core season of shed hunting, you may be left scratching your head. Maybe you've found a few sheds, but you thought you'd find more. There are a number of possible reasons why you weren't as successful as you'd hoped.

Ask yourself these questions about the area you shed hunted. Where did you focus your efforts? Is there a high deer population? What kind of hunting pressure does the area receive? Were other shed hunters working the same area? Have deer travel patterns changed in the area?

Obviously, the more deer there are, the better your odds of finding sheds, but look at the hunter harvest as well. If hunters shoot a lot of bucks, but few or no does in your area, you might still see a lot of deer, but you'll have trouble finding sheds because there are few bucks. A less-obvious problem is other shed hunters. Look for tracks in mud or snow, both from footprints and vehicles. You can be doing everything right, but if you're not the first shed-seeker in the area, you could be missing out.

Even if your selected area was a good one, did you search it effectively? Did you walk slowly and carefully? Were you distracted? Were you there before the antlers dropped? Did you pay attention to deer sign or just trail hop? There's an incredible temptation to just get on a deer trail and start walking, hopping from trail to trail as you find more well-used ones. Believe me, I think I invented that technique. It's true that you can find sheds on trails, especially if there are fences or other obstacles to jump, but in winter, a deer spends most of its time either feeding or bedding, and only a small percentage traveling. Swing the odds in your favor and try to analyze where deer are bedding and feeding and search those areas first.

Also, if you're in a likely looking area that you or someone else has already covered thoroughly, try something different. Remember, no one finds all the antlers. You may be able to find antlers if you skip the best-looking spots and hit the secondary areas. After all, a deer can drop an antler anywhere, and you never know when a buck will venture out of his core area for a brief excursion. Also, try approaching the woods from a different angle. There are countless stories of people who walked in a particular woodlot for years, only to find an old, faded antler they must have walked past dozens of times. Often a tree or other obstacle would have blocked your view of the shed in the direction you normally enter the woods. By entering somewhere else, or at least walking in the opposite direction you normally do, you'll see the woods differently and with fresh eyes.

Above all, remember, just because you hear of someone finding 100 sheds each season doesn't mean you should expect the same results. First off, find out what part of the world Mr. 100 Sheds is from. If he's finding his 100 sheds in the suburbs of Chicago and you live in the Upper Peninsula of Michigan where winters are tough and deer populations are low, there's probably a good reason why you're not keeping pace with Mr. 100 Sheds.

However, if you and Mr. 100 Sheds live in the same area, there's probably something you can do to help you find more antlers.

Just as in deer hunting, land access can be a factor for shed hunters. People with access to large landholdings of prime deer habitat usually have the best deer hunting, and that carries over to shed hunting somewhat, but not to the same degree. Access to quality private land is easier for shed hunters for several reasons. First, the landowner might hunt his own land for deer, but may have no time or interest in shed hunting. Or, he might lease his land to deer hunters. However, it's highly unlikely he leases the shed-hunting rights. (I've never heard of leasing shed-hunting rights, but cases are probably out there, or will be in the near future.) Also, farmers who have damaged farm equipment because of antlers may welcome shed hunters onto their property. It never hurts to ask.

Another major advantage shed hunters have over deer hunters is shed hunting can be done almost anywhere. Some of the best shed hunting is on public lands such as city or county parks, forest preserves or other areas open to the public but off-limits to hunting. This sort of levels the playing field for shed hunters.

Dealing With Competition

There are few things more frustrating than getting your hopes up for a long day of shedding, only to find a vehicle or fresh footprints in your favorite hotspot. As shed hunting becomes increasingly popular, competition for good shedding areas becomes steeper. Whereas the relatively few people who avidly sought antlers just a few years ago often had their favorite areas to themselves, nowadays some people go to great lengths to keep their hotspots hidden and to find antlers before anyone else can.

Keep in mind that your competition isn't just other shed hunters. Although they may be only casual shed hunters, and the antlers they find are only incidental, turkey hunters find many sheds each year. In the South, turkey seasons may start as early as February, when many bucks are still carrying their headgear.

Avoid parking where your vehicle can be easily seen to keep your best shed hunting spots a secret.

Farther north, seasons open right around the time the snow melts, revealing antlers that have been buried for weeks or months. When shed hunting in the spring, for your safety, keep in mind there could be turkey hunters in the woods. Also, make it a point to get out and look for antlers before turkey hunters have the chance.

There are several ways to deal with competing shed hunters, some of which are better solutions than others. One method is to simply hit the woods earlier. The early bird method does have merit, particularly if you know a certain buck has dropped its antlers. However, obviously, if you hit the woods in early January, hoping to find sheds before other people, you're going to miss the sheds from the bucks that are still packing their antlers. Then, you must either be satisfied with what you find on your first outing, or plan to make a return trip later. You also risk bumping a buck from his core area, and sending him off to drop his antlers somewhere else. Plus, if there is snow on the ground, you might also miss buried antlers, and your tracks will lead other shed seekers right to your best spots.

Savvy shed seekers don't let competition get them down. With perseverance and proper scouting, you can find sheds in heavily pressured areas.

If you expect other shed seekers to be out in force and don't have time to scour an area first, take what time you can spare and hit the best spots first. This gives you the opportunity to make the most valuable use of your time. Also, pick off the easy spots. Do give a thorough, but quick scan of an alfalfa field, where antlers should pop out at you, letting you cover the field with minimal walking, but don't waste precious time walking every row of a cornfield. Also, keep in mind most people will be doing their shed hunting on the weekend. Go out while you can during the week, and in particular, go out for an hour on Friday mornings, rather than Friday evenings when other people might already be out shedding for the weekend.

For example, one year in late March there was a foot of snow on the ground. The following Monday the temperature soared into the 60s, and the snow melted in a day or two. People I knew who weren't even avid shed hunters began stumbling onto antlers. I knew people would be out in droves on the weekend, so I made it a point to get out every evening that week, and even on my lunch break on some days. I searched the best areas first, such as farm fields on public ground that were newly exposed after the snow melted. This did two things. First, because these fields had been buried for months, it gave me the first crack at them. Second, while other people were out that weekend searching these same areas that I'd already covered, I moved on to other areas that hadn't been searched, keeping me in virgin territory as much as possible and maximizing my efforts.

You don't have to shed hunt long before learning that shed hunters are often quite protective of their hotspots. There are a number of things you can do to keep your spot a secret. For one thing, don't park your vehicle right next to where you're planning to shed hunt. You'll be doing a lot of walking anyway, so what's a little extra yardage? If possible, park somewhere where your vehicle will blend in with other vehicles, such as in a parking lot, in someone's driveway or even at a trout stream access point. You might even considering borrowing a friend or relative's vehicle if yours is well known or you're shed hunting in a rural area where everyone knows everyone else.

In the same manner, avoid revealing your shedding grounds by leaving footprints. If possible, don't leave tracks right on a public right-of-way. Rather, access the property from a less-obvious place if possible, or camouflage your tracks by avoiding snow or mud. Depending on the area, you may be able to access the area from a side road, bike trail or a neighbor's property. I've been known to wade a trout stream, walk on top of logs and even scratch out my tracks with a stick to keep my presence a secret. Also, pay attention to the weather. If the forecast calls for precipitation, you can time a shed hunt just right so that rain or snow will cover up your tracks.

Leaving behind tracks isn't always a bad thing. Sometimes tracks can be used defensively. For example, if you know other people shed hunt the same areas you do, you can track it all up in an attempt to discourage people from searching there, even if you haven't had adequate time to search it yourself. Some people even wear different pairs of boots in an area to give the impression that more than one person has already been through the place. Perhaps if you've really made a name for yourself as an accomplished local shed hunter, you may even be able to mislead the competition by parking your truck in a very visible area or tracking up a less-than-ideal area. While other folks think they are keying in on your secret spot, you'll actually be raking in the antlers at your actual shed haven.

Finding evidence that other people have been hunting "your" spot is disappointing, but all is not lost. Granted, antlers may have been removed from the most obvious places, but there's always a strong possibility that some were left behind. You just have to be willing to search longer and harder than the people before you. Perhaps hit the less-obvious spots and see what you can come up with. And remember, there's always the possibility that a buck has shed since the spot was last searched. I always remind myself that a buck could have dropped an antler 5 minutes ago in any given place. This helps me keep a positive attitude. If you've got a negative outlook, you're more likely to give a sub-par effort. If that happens, you're just wasting your time.

Remember, just because you find someone else shed hunting in one of your preferred shedding locales, all is not lost. Shed hunters tend to be good-hearted, friendly folks, even if a bit secretive and sometimes deceptive. You may run across another shed seeker and discover he has the match to an antler you found. You might work out a trade, and form more than a matched set; you might form a valuable shed-hunting partnership or even find a new hunting buddy.

Shed-Hunting Partnerships and Ethics

One of the nicest gestures a shed hunter can make is to invite you to shed hunt in a favorite spot. If the individual is serious about shed hunting, this invitation should not be taken lightly.

A shed-hunting relationship is sort of like a marriage in that both require a lot of trust. I point this out not because I enjoy lecturing readers, but because

STICKER POINT:

Attitude

Cross-examine a group of successful shed hunters and you're sure to find some similarities between them. In addition to good eyesight, a near obsession with deer and probably a lot of free time in late winter and spring, you'll almost certainly find that every single one of them possesses a positive attitude. It's simple: If you walk into the woods doubting any bucks survived the hunting season and believing you're wasting your time, then you surely are. You stand almost no chance of finding any sheds and you won't enjoy your time afield. As soon as you convince yourself that you won't find sheds, you've lost.

Attitude truly is everything, whether you're a baseball player trying to break out of a hitting slump or a shed seeker trying to see that first glint of antler in two weeks. If you leave the truck with a negative attitude, your senses become dull. Your eyes will bounce right over a tine tip and you'll become too complacent to take a few extra steps to double-check the identity of sticks that resemble antlers. You're more likely to become distracted and your thoughts will wander. A former coach used to tell me when I put in a lousy effort at practice, "With that kind of effort, you might as well take a bar of soap and scrub yourself in the locker room because that's all you'll get for your effort." If you reach that point, you need to either pause and re-focus or admit defeat because you're in no position to find an antler.

No one likes a braggart, and no good can come from bragging about what you've found. Granted, being selfish is no better than bragging, but it avoids a lot of problems. Therefore, it's wise to be careful about whom you show your sheds to and whom you tell about your shedding grounds. As soon as you show off your sheds, you'll have people asking questions about your shed-hunting and deer-hunting grounds and things can turn messy in a hurry. Rather, share information with only those you trust, such as close hunting partners and people in your tight shed-hunting network, or you're likely to end up with more competition in your honey holes.

sometimes people break the rules of common courtesy, whether they intended to hone in on someone else's spot, or whether they innocently failed to realize that sharing shed-hunting grounds called for trust and respect. More than one friendship has been fouled up by antlers, which is absolutely silly. Shed hunting is about having fun and spending time outside. It should not be a wedge between friends.

In order to allay any possible negative experiences, it's good to lay the ground rules on the table before leaving the truck. It's generally accepted that if two people shed hunting together each find an antler from the same buck, whoever found the first side keeps both sheds. This doesn't have to be *your* rule, but *some* rule should be established beforehand to prevent any problems. This also means if you are invited along to find a specific antler that your friend already has the match to, if you find the matching antler, no matter how big it is, it's not yours to keep. This can be a tough pill to swallow, especially when you walk up on the biggest shed of your life and have to give it away, but good deeds have a way of being rewarded.

Another good idea when shed hunting in a group is to call out an antler as soon as you see it so there will be no disputing who found it. One shed hunter I know, Tom, has been victimized by this situation a few times. The first time, he and a friend spied a nice moose paddle at the same time. They couldn't decide who should keep it, so their best compromise was to cut the tines off, with one person keeping the tines and the other keeping the palm – not a very good compromise if you ask me. The second time he spotted the biggest shed he'd ever found one day while working in the woods. Before he could find the words, his boss yelled, "There's a shed!" and Tom had to listen to his boss' story the rest of the day about the big shed "he" found.

Also, it's common courtesy to only go to your friend's spot with your friend. You should not go there without him or her, and you certainly shouldn't invite your buddies, your neighbor and your in-laws along. You should respect landowners' rights and stay out of areas where they don't want you. Keep gates locked, don't litter and leave the place better than you found it. It's always a nice gesture to throw some hay bales around or help with other chores when you're shed hunting on a farm as well.

Having a close shed-hunting partner can be a real joy. Two people can cover more ground, put their heads together to unravel the travel patterns of a specific deer and share information that will help them find more sheds as a team. A pair of shed-seekers can more easily cover a field from an ATV with one person driving and the other free to look for antlers. A buddy can also be a great asset if you twist your ankle a mile from the truck. Plus, it's just a lot more fun to have someone to share the shed-hunting experience with. With that said, pick your shed-hunting friends carefully. If you don't think you can trust them with your best shed-hunting spot, don't show them. It's as simple as that.

How Do You Rate?

After you've shed hunted for a while, and hopefully enjoyed some success, you might find yourself wondering just how good of a shed hunter you are. Are other people finding more than you, or less than you? And how many other shed hunters are out there?

A poll posted by the Iowa Whitetails Web site (www.iowawhitetail.com) may "shed" some light on the subject. I suppose it's human nature to compare yourself to the next guy, and the poll did just that. The question was "How many sheds do you find each year?" This question was posted for several months in spring 2005. There were six choices to select. The results were as follows:

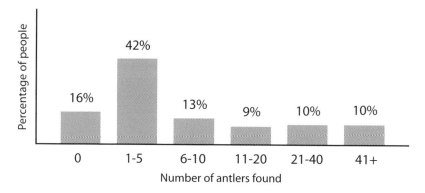

HOW MANY SHEDS DO YOU FIND EACH YEAR?

Is this a formal, scientific survey depicting an accurate cross-reference of the shed-hunting community? No, but it's probably a pretty good indication. I would suspect that as deer hunters go, only a small percentage find sheds each year. But as far as shed hunters go – people who actually make an attempt to find antlers in the spring – the poll may be fairly accurate. It shows that 58 percent of the folks are probably casual shed hunters who find five or fewer sheds each year. Those 32

The North American Shed Hunters Club shed-antler museum contains an impressive collection of large and unusual antlers from several species.

percent who find from six to 40 sheds per year are pretty good shed hunters, and those who find more than that are absolute fanatics!

The Iowa Whitetails Web Site is an excellent place to learn more about shed hunting by participating in the online shed-hunting forum. On it you'll find many other shed hunters, who love to discuss shed hunting and share advice with other shed addicts.

North American Shed Hunters Club

The North American Shed Hunters Club Web site (www.shedantlers.org) also has great shed-hunting forums set up specifically for deer, moose, elk and more. In fact, some serious shed hunters see the forum as a sort of support group to help them endure those months when sheds are buried by snow or lush grass! The NASHC also has links to places where you can book shed hunts and other antler-related links.

The NASHC was formed in Minnesota in 1991, before shed hunting was really on the radar screen as a pastime. Now located in Wisconsin, the organization has grown as more people become interested in shedding. NASHC promotes shed hunting as a great way to introduce kids and adults to the outdoors. The club's national headquarters houses a shed antler museum with hundreds of large, small and unusual shed antlers of various species. NASHC also keeps track of shed antler records for all species of North American antlered big game in four categories: single antler typical, single antler nontypical, matched set typical and matched set nontypical. The club scores antlers using the Boone & Crockett scoring system. Minimum entry scores for whitetail sheds are 60 inches for a typical antler and 70 inches for a nontypical. Matched set minimums are double the single-entry minimums. Chewed and weathered antlers are allowed in the record book, as long as the integrity of the shed remains intact.

Visitors to the NASHC national convention can enter their antlers into the big shed contest.

SHED ANTLER RECORDS OF NORTH AMERICAN BIG GAME®

North American Shed Hunters Club®
PO BOX 339 - 166 Wisconsin St.
Lyndon Station, WI 53944
Ph: (608) 666-2071
E-mail: nashinfo@shedantlers.org
Web Page: www.shedantlers.org
web sheet

MINIMUM ENTRY SCORES FOR ONE SIDE BOTH TYPICAL & NON-TYP.
Mule Deer - 65 inches Typ - 75 inches Non. Typ.
Whitetail Deer - 60 inches Typ - 70 inches Non. Typ.
Columbia Blacktail - 40 inches Typ - 45 inches Non. Typ.
Sitka Blacktail - 30 inches Typ - 35 inches Non. Typ.
Coues' Whitetail - 25 inches Typ - 30 inches Non. Typ.

OFFICIAL SCORE AND REGISTRATION SHEET FOR THE NORTH AMERICAN SHED HUNTERS CLUB

Date Measured: Exact Type of Animal:	Items To Measure	COL - 1 Right Antler Scores	COL - 2 Left Antler Scores	COL - 3 Side To Side Difference	COL - 4 Abnormal Points Right - Left	
A. Total Inches of Col. 1 _____	Main Beams					
B. Total Inches of Col. 2 _____	G-1					
C. Sub-Total = _____	G-2					
D. Subtract Col 3 -- _____	G-3					
E. Total In. Col. 1 & 2 = _____	G-4					
F. Add or Subtract Col. 4 _____	G-5					
G. Net Final Score = _____	G-6					
H. Year Shed(s) Found: _____	G-7					
I. State/Province From: _____	C-1					
J. Found By: _____	C-2					
K. High Fence Shed(s) Yes No	C-3					
Please do not include single entries and matched pairs on the same score sheets						
Remarks:	C-4					
	Total Inches:					

PLEASE PRINT CLEARLY

Owner's Name: _____ Address: _____ City:_____

State/Province: _____ Zip/PC: _____ Ph: ( )_____

Measurer's Name: _____ Address: _____ City: _____

State/Province: _____ Zip/PC: _____ Ph: ( )_____

NASHC Measurer's I.D.# _____ Measuring Club or State Affiliation: _____

AFFIDAVIT OF ENTRY

In making this entry, I Certify that I found, traded or purchased this entry legally, and that it was not obtained by trespassing on a reservation, government or private property, game farm, State or National Park, hunting preserve or wildlife sanctuary without permission, consent or permission from the land owner, resident lessee, caretaker or conservation officer. I also certify that this entry was found, or came from, the geographical boundaries for which this species is recognized.

Owner's Signature: _____ **Date:** _____

This sample score sheet was provided by the NASHC. You can find an official score sheet at www.shedantlers.org.

NASHC sets up booths at major deer shows throughout the country and holds its annual national convention each April. The two-day event features antler displays, a big-shed contest, exhibitors and more. Plus, it's a good place to meet other shed hunters, many of whom get to meet face to face after discussing shed hunting for months on the NASHC Internet forum. For more information about the club, contact:

NASHC
P.O. Box 339
Lyndon Station, WI 53944
(608) 666-2071
www.shedantlers.org

8
Antler Roundup

What you do with your antlers after you find them is up to you. Mine end up sitting around on shelves or tables where I can look at them and play with them when the mood strikes, but if you're artistically inclined (and can bear the thought of altering antlers from their natural state), you can make some beautiful projects with antlers. Traditionally, antlers were used for such things as making knife handles, flint knapping, in ceremonial dances and for many other uses. They were, and still are, even ground into powder as an aphrodisiac. Today, antler products are as popular as ever. One of the most popular and traditional items is the antler chandelier. If your collection of sheds is large enough, you may be able to make your own chandelier, or have a professional chandelier maker produce one with your sheds. If your collection isn't that large, consider making an antler lamp. Other projects allow you to make multiple projects from one antler. Cross-sections of antlers are used to make buttons, main beams and tines are fastened to doors for decorative handles and small sections of antler tines tip fireplace tools. Plus, antlers give a rustic, decorative touch to book shelves, coat racks, towel holders, lamps, baskets,

◀ *Antler crafts are just one of the many uses for shed antlers.*

cribbage boards or even furniture. Pieces of antlers can be used to make drawer pulls, and large antler bases can be made into belt buckles. If nothing else, you can use your sheds for rattling up bucks during hunting season. Uses for shed antlers are endless; it's the supply that's not.

If you're lucky enough to find an especially nice matched set that has special meaning to you, you could have a taxidermist install the sheds on a shoulder mount. This is a great way to display sheds, and the only real way to "do them justice" to see how they would really look on a buck's head.

Most any taxidermist should be able to mount sheds on a shoulder mount. All that's required is a cape, and from there the taxidermist mounts the antlers on a form, using the best estimate for positioning and width of the spread. One interesting aspect of the mount idea is that you may be able to have a mount

You can mount a matched set of sheds on "shed connectors," such as this product from Van Dyke's Taxidermy (www.vandykestaxidermy.com). After you secure a deer cape the sheds can then be incorporated into a shoulder mount.

Antlers give a rustic ambience to any home.

created that lets you remove the antlers, so you can still examine the sheds individually. The taxidermist drills into the base of the antlers, then inserts a metal rod. The shoulder mount has a corresponding hole that accommodates the rod. This removable antler system is often employed on large game heads such as elk, because it makes it much easier to transport the mount and maneuver it through your house.

Taxidermy supply catalogs also sell "shed connectors" These devices serve the same function as a skull plate. Depending on the type, some connectors are adjustable and allow you to position the antlers at the angle and width you deem right for the particular buck. Other units that are molded from the actual skull plate of a buck are also available. In either case you drill a hole into the base of the sheds, insert a screw and then you have the option of applying epoxy if you want to attach the sheds permanently. Shed connectors can be used when creating a shoulder mount, or simply to perform a traditional skull plate mount.

Shedding for Fun and Profit

Antlers have special meaning to those who find them. Seeing them sitting on a shelf reminds us of good times in the woods. For those lucky enough to find

Nathan Danz of Montana designed this unique antler coat rack.

multiple sheds from the same buck, or put a deer tag on a buck they have sheds to, those sheds become extra special. But if you can bear to part with your antlers, you may be surprised at the price shed antlers can fetch.

You can find antlers for sale in many places, such as garage sales, flea markets, antique stores, sports shows and on the Internet. And, as rustic décor becomes more popular in cabins and homes, more companies deal in natural "art," including shed antlers, and some companies deal in antlers exclusively. If you do an Internet search for "shed antler," you'll be amazed at all the places you can find sheds, and eBay may be one of the most notable. This online auction lists dozens of sheds daily, and some of them are truly world class.

If you're looking to sell your sheds, you might consider selling them to an antler dealer, or you could put them up for bid on eBay. You might even be able to sell directly to artisans who use antlers to carve or make knife handles, door pulls or the like. Watching auction sales and antler prices online is a good way to get a feel for what your sheds are worth.

Antlers are generally lumped into a few condition categories that determine pricing. Fresh, brown antlers with no chew marks command the best prices. They have the most value to collectors and artists.

Sheds that are bleached white, but still in good condition make the second grade. From a carving standpoint these antlers are still sound and valuable, but

Small or flawed antlers are great materials for craft projects.

their discoloration may make them less desirable for some applications. Fresh antlers with some chewing would probably also rank in this category, depending on the extent of the chewing.

Cracked, white antlers rank next. Their porous, chalky nature makes them largely unappealing for decorations, but they may still be suitable for carving.

Heavily chewed antlers and green antlers are usually of little value unless they are of exceptional size.

Antlers, like any commodity, are worth only what someone will pay you. Your first shed is intrinsically more valuable to you than to an antler buyer, especially if it's small. Obviously, the larger the antler, the more it's generally worth, with condition being taken into consideration. A 100-inch cracked white antler should fetch more than a 75-inch brown antler. Obviously, an 80-inch fresh brown antler should fetch more than an 80-inch cracked white antler.

The antler's configuration may also have some bearing on its value. Unusual features such as drop tines, double main beams and heavy palmation are uncommon and can add value to an antler. Sheds will also be more valuable when sold as a matched set. Exceptional size plays a role in price determination as well.

A 70-inch 4-point antler may be more valuable to some than a 70-inch 5-point shed, simply because the 4-pointer must have exceptional mass, tine length or both to total up to such an impressive figure.

Smaller antlers are often sold in bunches, and their price is usually on a per-pound basis. Larger sheds are typically sold alone or as matched sets. Larger antlers are more valuable per pound. For example, a 20-pound lot of 30 small antlers would likely cost less than a 20-pound lot consisting of 15 larger antlers. It's quality that counts. You may also be able to sell your antlers in pieces. Someone making antler knife handles is only interested in the larger main beam. However, someone who makes buttons may be interested in buying the thinner-diameter tines.

I do not sell antlers I've found and have no intention of doing so. Each antler I find is a unique artifact that holds special meaning to me. However, if you're planning to sell your sheds, there are definitely markets for them, from crafters to collectors. It's just a matter of finding someone who wants to buy what you are selling.

Antler Repair

The fields and forests that deer call home can be rough places to live if you're a deer, but they're even more inhospitable to antlers. Even if an antler survives an autumn of head-to-head clashes with other bucks, it can become squirrel food the moment it hits the ground. Sometimes the sheds you pick up aren't in perfect shape. That leaves you three choices, or only two if you don't feel like shooting squirrels. You can either leave the shed as you found it, with battle scars intact, or try to restore it.

With a little artistic skill and a lot of time, you can make a chewed or broken antler look original. Obviously, the smaller the imperfection, the easier it will be to repair. A few chew marks can be patched up much easier than you could replace a broken tine or snapped-off main beam. But for those with some artistic skills – and a lot of ambition – pretty much anything is possible, even creating a matching antler to a shed you found from scratch!

Before you try repairing one of your prized sheds, I'd recommend practicing on an old "junk" antler until you get the hang of antler repair. You certainly don't want to mess up the first time. However, another reason for practicing is finding a repair method that works for you. Most people repair antlers in the same general manner, but there are so many variations regarding which materials to use, how to stain (or not to stain) and other details. I'd recommend talking to a taxidermist

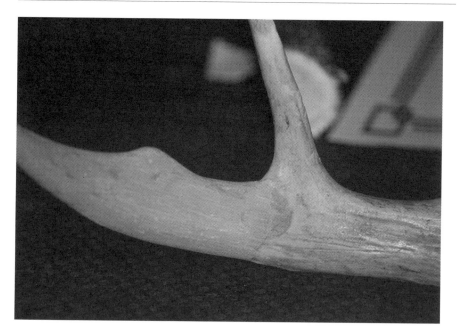

You can repair minor flaws or even create an entire antler with auto body filler or specially made antler repair putty.

and getting first-hand advice from a pro, then practicing on your own. Here are the guidelines I've come to learn for antler repair.

Let's say you've got a shed with a broken-off tine that you want to restore from scratch. If you've got the matching antler, you can get a good feel for tine length, otherwise you'll have to guess how long the tine should be.

Start by drilling a hole a half-inch deep into the base of the broken-off point. You'll be inserting sturdy wire (such as coat-hanger wire) into the hole, so choose a bit diameter a little wider than your wire. Next, insert the wire into the hole and cut it off a little shorter than your desired tine length. Epoxy the wire into the hole.

Here's where the variances begin. The goal now is to form the shape of the tine with some sort of substance that can be easily formed but dries hard. Some people use auto body filler, while others use special putty from taxidermy supply catalogs made specifically for recreating antlers. One of the most commonly used methods involves Apoxie Sculpt modeling compound and Epo-Grip antler-repair putty. You can actually use either or both of these products together, but they seem to work well in combinations, so I'll describe techniques using both products.

Begin by forming the shape of the antler tine with Apoxie Sculpt. You can buy it from taxidermy shops and even craft stores. Remember to form the tine larger than you want it so you can sand it and add scratches, veins, beading or other realistic details.

After you've formed the tine with Apoxie Sculpt, file it down to the desired size and shape, and add any natural details mentioned above. When you're satisfied, sand it lightly. Next, apply a thin layer of Epo-Grip putty. This product takes stain well and forms a nice finish, but beware that it dries fast and you'll have to work with it quickly. Once the Epo-Grip has cured, it's time to put the finishing touches on your work. Sand the antler with fine-grit sandpaper. Then, color the antler using wood stain, oil paints or specially made antler stains. Start with lighter colors and light coats and gradually build to a darker color. Remember, antler bases tend to be darker, tine tips are lighter and the main beam and other parts of antler tines are somewhere in between. When you've achieved the desired hue, buff with a soft cloth, rub it with beeswax for a natural sheen and buff again.

The Off-Season

For true shed hunters, there is no off-season. Although tall grass and dense

Johnray Vance of Ohio has devised this display rack for some of his sheds.

Shed hunting is a great way to introduce people to the outdoors.

foliage makes it hard to find sheds in the summer and fall, you'll never find all the antlers, so it's not impossible to find sheds at these times. However, even if you're not actively looking for antlers on the ground, you can scout for the upcoming shedding season by monitoring deer movements, surveying the bucks living in your area and seeking new places to shed hunt. Many – but not all – shed hunters also hunt deer, so keeping tabs on deer isn't a problem. In fact, if you're really into shed hunting, you may pause before you pull the trigger on a buck, because you know that doing so will keep you from finding two antlers in the spring! It sounds crazy, but I admit I do think about it ... but not for very long.

Summer, fall and early winter are great times to make antler crafts, rearrange your collection or have a get-together with fellow shed hunters to swap stories and show off the season's finds. It's also a good time to start training a shed-hunting dog.

If you're really suffering from "sheditis," that withdrawal one gets after months of not shed hunting, which is often characterized by involuntary drooling whenever you see an antler, know that there are cures. There are some great shed-hunting videos out there that take you back to those spring days we all dream about. Doug Coleman currently has three videos in his *Through the Eyes of a Shed Hunter* series, and Bentley Coben has produced a video entitled *Treasures in the Buck Brush*. You can contact Doug at dtcoleman@cableone.net or Bentley at www.bentleycoben.com.

Wrap-Up

Shed hunting is becoming more popular every year, and for good reason. It's a great way to scout for deer, spend time outside and introduce people to the outdoors. Looking for antlers teaches you woodsmanship and deer behavior. Pay attention to what's going on in the woods and you will learn something new every time out, and in time, you'll witness some bizarre things.

Once you've learned the basics of how deer feed, bed and travel, you'll be able to find sheds anywhere. Each geographic area certainly has its own nuances, but there are a lot of universal deer behaviors. Deer have to eat, sleep and travel wherever they live. In time you may try to find antlers in other states or provinces, or even try for sheds from mule deer, moose, elk and caribou.

Wherever you go, keep your eyes on the ground and good luck!

References

Alsheimer, Charles J. *Whitetail Behavior Through the Seasons*. Iola, Wis.: Krause Publications, 1996.

American Podiatric Medical Association, personal contact, November 2005.

Bubenik, George A. and Anthony B. *Horns, Pronghorns, and Antlers: Evolution, Morphology, Physiology and Social Significance*. New York: Springer-Verlag, 1990.

Goss, Dr. Richard J. *Deer Antlers: Regeneration, Function and Evolution*. New York: Academic Press, 1983.

Hampton, Walt. "Japanese Honeysuckle: Deer Food or Forest Pest?" *Deer & Deer Hunting*, June 2001, pp. 63-64.

Ozoga, John J. *John Ozoga's Whitetail Intrigue*. Edited by Patrick Durkin. Iola, Wis.: Krause Publications, 2000.

_____. *Whitetail Winter*. Minocqua, Wis.: Willow Creek Press, 1995.

_____. Telephone Interview, Aug. 3, 2006

Rue III, Dr. Leonard Lee. *The Encyclopedia of Deer*. Stillwater, Minn.: Voyageur Press, 2003.

Severinghaus, C.W. and A.N. Moen. 1983. "Prediction of Weight and Reproductive Rates of White-tailed Deer Population from Records of Antler Beam Diameter Among Yearling Deer." *New York Fish and Game Journal* 30(1)30-38.

North American Shed Hunters Club (www.shedantlers.org)

Iowa Whitetail (www.iowawhitetail.com)

www.webmd.com

Index

A

acorns 37
alfalfa 37, 74
algal growth 91-92, 144
American Podiatric Medical Association 48
ankle sprain 50
antler growth 17, 18, 20
antler repair 145-147
antler stripper 112
arch pain 50
apples 37
athlete's foot 49
ATV 78, 110-111

B

bachelor group 30, 82, 108
base 16, 61, 88
beam diameter 100-101
bed 27, 29, 30, 35, 65
big woods 82, 84
binoculars 46, 75, 78
bleached 91-92, 103-104, 143
blisters 49
blood trailing 85
bone 14, 15
boots 46-47
border information 120-121
brassica 112
browse 33, 36, 38
burr 16, 88

C

calcium 18, 22, 23, 90
Canadian shed hunt 117-122
cancer IX

Coben, Bentley and Dianne VII, 122, 148
Coleman, Doug and Tammy VII, 54, 116-118, 148
competition 127-132
corn 35, 37, 38, 61, 76, 112
corns and calluses 50
crafts 140-142, 148
creeping cedar 37-39
crop fields 74-78

D
deer yard 34, 97
dogs 114-118, 148
droppings 30

E
eBay 143
equipment 45-46

F
fading 89
food plots 37, 112
foot care 47-50
funnel 84

G
golden rules 55
gonadotrophin 18
Goss, Richard VIII
GPS 46, 108
grid search 67
guided shed hunt 119-122

H
hanger 66
health indices 99
hormone 18, 22
horns IX, 14, 17

I

infant antlers 17
Iowa Whitetails 136

J

Japanese honeysuckle 40
journal 104-106, 108-109

K

keratin 14, 17
kinesthetic sense 19

L

latitude 24
Lyme disease 50-51

M

matched set 87, 92-98
melatonin 18
mounting 142

N

North American Shed Hunters Club VII, XII, 136-139

O

osteoclast 22

P

partnerships 132-135
pedicel 17, 18
phosphorous 18, 90
pits and spicules 22, 23
private land 68-71
public land 69, 71-73

R

red maple 37-38

rubs 21, 27, 65, 82, 84
rut 23, 27, 30
rye 37, 114

S
scouting cameras 94, 96
seal depth 100
selling antlers 142-145
shed connectors 142
shedding process 22
skin ring 16, 88, 89
snow country 82-83
social status 22, 23
socks 46
south-facing slope 31, 38, 76, 103, 108
squirrel 66, 90, 92, 113
staging areas 40
suburbs 123-125
T
testosterone 18, 20, 22, 28, 99
ticks 50-51
tines up/down 61-62
tossing antler 63-64
tractor tire 69

U
urban areas 68, 123-125
U.S. Fish and Wildlife Service 121

V
velvet 19-21
Veterinary Health Certificate of Export of Cervid Antlers to the U.S. 121

W
weather 67, 84, 90
white cedar 34, 37, 38, 40

Shed Hunting Log

Date: _____ **Side:** R L **Points:** _____ **Score:** _____

Location: _____

Orientation: Up Down **Age:** Fresh Old

How Shed: (circle) Bedding Feeding Walking Jumping Rubbing Unknown

Details: _____
_____
_____

Date: _____ **Side:** R L **Points:** _____ **Score:** _____

Location: _____

Orientation: Up Down **Age:** Fresh Old

How Shed: (circle) Bedding Feeding Walking Jumping Rubbing Unknown

Details: _____
_____
_____

Date: _____ **Side:** R L **Points:** _____ **Score:** _____

Location: _____

Orientation: Up Down **Age:** Fresh Old

How Shed: (circle) Bedding Feeding Walking Jumping Rubbing Unknown

Details: _____
_____
_____

Shed Hunting Log

Date: _____   **Side:** R   L   **Points:** _____   **Score:** _____

Location: _____

Orientation: Up   Down   **Age:** Fresh   Old

How Shed: (circle) Bedding   Feeding   Walking   Jumping   Rubbing   Unknown

Details: _____

_____

_____

Date: _____   **Side:** R   L   **Points:** _____   **Score:** _____

Location: _____

Orientation: Up   Down   **Age:** Fresh   Old

How Shed: (circle) Bedding   Feeding   Walking   Jumping   Rubbing   Unknown

Details: _____

_____

_____

Date: _____   **Side:** R   L   **Points:** _____   **Score:** _____

Location: _____

Orientation: Up   Down   **Age:** Fresh   Old

How Shed: (circle) Bedding   Feeding   Walking   Jumping   Rubbing   Unknown

Details: _____

_____

_____

Shed Hunting Log

Date: _____ **Side:** R L **Points:** _____ **Score:** _____

Location: _____

Orientation: Up Down **Age:** Fresh Old

How Shed: (circle) Bedding Feeding Walking Jumping Rubbing Unknown

Details: _____
_____
_____

Date: _____ **Side:** R L **Points:** _____ **Score:** _____

Location: _____

Orientation: Up Down **Age:** Fresh Old

How Shed: (circle) Bedding Feeding Walking Jumping Rubbing Unknown

Details: _____
_____
_____

Date: _____ **Side:** R L **Points:** _____ **Score:** _____

Location: _____

Orientation: Up Down **Age:** Fresh Old

How Shed: (circle) Bedding Feeding Walking Jumping Rubbing Unknown

Details: _____
_____
_____

Shed Hunting Log

Date: _____ **Side:** R L **Points:** _____ **Score:** _____

Location: _____

Orientation: Up Down **Age:** Fresh Old

How Shed: (circle) Bedding Feeding Walking Jumping Rubbing Unknown

Details: _____

_____

_____

Date: _____ **Side:** R L **Points:** _____ **Score:** _____

Location: _____

Orientation: Up Down **Age:** Fresh Old

How Shed: (circle) Bedding Feeding Walking Jumping Rubbing Unknown

Details: _____

_____

_____

Date: _____ **Side:** R L **Points:** _____ **Score:** _____

Location: _____

Orientation: Up Down **Age:** Fresh Old

How Shed: (circle) Bedding Feeding Walking Jumping Rubbing Unknown

Details: _____

_____

_____

Anything for an antler!